CITY LEVELS

BIRKHÄUSER – PUBLISHERS FOR ARCHITECTURE
BASEL · BOSTON · BERLIN

AUGUST, LONDON

A CIP catalogue record for this book is available from the Library of Congress, Washington D.C., USA

Deutsche Bibliothek Cataloging-in-Publication Data

City levels / Nick Barley and Ally Ireson (ed.). - Basel ; Boston ; Berlin : Birkhäuser, 2000
ISBN 3-7643-6315-0

© 2000 Birkhäuser –
Publishers for Architecture,
P.O. Box 133, CH-4010 Basel,
Switzerland.
August Media Ltd,
116–120 Golden Lane,
London EC1Y OTL, UK

Printed on acid-free paper produced of chlorine-free pulp. TCF ∞

ISBN 3-7643-6315-0

9 8 7 6 5 4 3 2 1

Editors: Ally Ireson and Nick Barley
Art director: Anne Odling-Smee
Creative director: Stephen Coates

Production co-ordinated by:
Uwe Kraus GmbH

Printed in Italy

Publisher's acknowledgements:
Liam Bailey, Fiona Bradley, the staff of the British Airways London Eye, Andy Carver, Diana Eggenschwiler, Darren Flook at Entwistle, Hannah Ford, Laura Henderson, Jonathan Heaf, Nigel Jackson, Niall O'Leary at Millennium Images, Katie Pratt at Edelman, Silke Roch, Elisabeth Scheder-Bieschin, Robert Steiger, Alex Stetter, Rachel Taylor

IN THE AGE OF
HORIZONTALIZATION
OLE BOUMAN

If there is one thing that has survived consecutive paradigm shifts throughout the history of architecture, it is the metaphorical value of height. Whether the classical, the modern or the postmodern, architecture served the metaphysics of verticalism. The Vitruvian orders, the Miesian skyscraper, even the symbolist narrativism of pomo's object-oriented monumentality: looking up to architecture has meant in some way a moral uplifting to higher values.

Apart from multiplying the groundplan, height used to be a sign of transcendence. Now we are entering an age in which height can no longer rely on its hierarchical meaning. An architectural construction goes up, while we stay down to earth, in an ongoing emphasis on the relativity of all moral constructs.

What does elevation mean in an age of horizontalization of world views? The vertical, according to Aristotle, was the meeting of a

human being with his/her shadow. This lies at the root of an idealistic paradigm, in which there is a basic difference between the real and the unreal, in which the first rules the second. Architecture has been the perfect vehicle with which to convey this idea. But, if this paradigm crumbles, we still have elevation. We still have angles of 90 degrees. But they lose their metaphysical power.

So the question is whether architecture as a cultural medium can survive the loss of the top-down power system justification. And the answer lies in approaching its meaning in another dimension than the one of construction. This could mean the ultimate detachment of architecture and building and the rise of architecture as pure environment. If there is no moral superiority to be found on the 40th floor anymore, there is still experience possible there.

Perhaps one thing should be fully considered now: it is no longer lonely at the top.

INTRODUCTION
ALLY IRESON

'We live in cities badly; we have built them up in culpable innocence and now fret helplessly in a synthetic wilderness of our own construction. We need – more urgently than architectural uptopias, ingenious traffic disposal systems, or ecological programmes – to comprehend the nature of citizenship, to make a serious imaginative reassessment of that special relationship between the self and the city; its unique plasticity.'
Jonathan Raban

An aerial photograph of Manhattan, taken on 5 July 1940 by the US Coast and Geodetic Survey. Taken at an angle, the picture turns New York's famous skyscrapers into a forest of regimented, geometric stalagmites: a city exploding out of a grid of streets that dissolve in deep shadow. Devoid of the distracting signs of everyday life, the city is instantly iconic. Although the bristling black and white image is over sixty years out of date, it looks like a snapshot of modernity. Chiming with an idea of the city that still seems to hold the affection of much of the contemporary world, the photograph is all vertiginous exhilaration and architectural exclamation marks – an index of our persistent passion for tall buildings. It is difficult not to be seduced by all those thrusting blocks; by their audacity, the way they seem to express a very human ambition to make a mark, to punch strong steel, glass and brick statements into the flat plane of the ground. Whichever version of urban reality we actually live in, most of us recognise the Manhattan of the photograph as a pattern for our Superlative City, one owing much of its charisma to vertical energy.

New York and lesser skylines the world over stand testament to the twentieth century's focus on building upwards, and even as we enter a new one, the pace of vertical architecture doesn't look set to slacken. In the past decade, a dizzying sequence of towers have been constructed in the fast-developing cities of the Pacific Rim, as the East plays an aspirational game of catch up with the West. Our enduring interest in how far and how fast the newest monumental building will climb skywards (the media's thirst for the 'next tallest' has often forced premature statements about completion dates from developers) is informed by a general disinterest in the less immediately visible zones of our cities, the ones which exist between the tops of buildings, the pavement and beyond; the thoroughly localised elements which form the backdrop to everyday life: expressways, doorways, underground stations, low-rise housing, schools, shopping centres, side streets, roof-tops, offices, rail depots, industrial estates, supermarkets.

Unlike the Eiffel Tower, Nelson's Column and the Empire State – what could be the emphatic tent poles of a more transcendent urban vision – these more anonymous zones are hard to turn into a postcard. A conventional emphasis on the highest points as the defining aspect of cities can mean that much is missed. For example, a ride on London's new giant Ferris Wheel (see page 15) – officially the 'London Eye' – sees many passengers turn towards the scattered towers of the City of London and the Docklands area to gain a fitting view of 'the capital city'. Somehow, the lower-level stone and glass cliffs of the West End don't have as much potency. It seems that from the elevated perspective offered by the glass capsules, we want a city to make

Above: in what seems a neat reminder of the relativity of the term 'tallest', it is currently possible to overlook the top of the world's highest building from another building: the hilly landscape surrounding Kuala Lumpur means that a television tower on the edge of the city is a good vantage point from which to see Cesar Pelli's Petronas Towers.
Opposite: Berlin's Marienkirche and Teletower.

large claims for itself. But eyes only tuned to height miss many more subtle indications of the life of the city, such as the intimacy of a table set for breakfast on a single, tiny balcony of the former Greater London Council building on the south side of the Thames.

City Levels argues that is not by concentrating on the most immediately emphatic parts of a city that we can necessarily make the best sense of it. The book suggests that to do so also requires an engagement with the more anonymous zones by making an imaginative exploration of four different territories defined by the distance at which they exist above or below the zero height of the pavement. That a city is a layered environment is self-evident to those people who live in one. Every day, we negotiate often complex routes up, down and through a series of architectural and geographical layers. And even if we don't have to move very far to go about our ordinary business, a short walk at street level can demonstrate the fact we are moving through a dense and complex space, as the distant (and more readily iconic) city made up of the tops of church spires and towerblocks constantly slides in and out of view behind buildings. Similarly, in most modern cities, we are made aware of another layer beneath the concrete skin of pedestrian level, as we descend escalators and flights of stairs into underground transport systems, car parks or storage spaces. However, although we may all be well versed in the up-and-down rules of urban life, it is a challenge to rethink our perspective on the significance of the vertical zones they index as contexts for specific patterns of architectural design, or types of interaction between people, or people and the city itself.

City Levels proposes to take an interest in verticality, but only as an axis along which to view the city in a different way. Taking slices through the urban fabric in cross-section, the book treats it as a stack of interconnected horizontal levels, rather than as a series of buildings plugged into the ground with valueless space hanging above, below and in-between. The book's four chapters: focusing on 'the highest point', 'elevated territories', 'the street' and 'beneath ground', aim to give voice to a rich, fluid and multi-layered urban reality that cannot be described by a conventional map. It also seeks to open up territories previously hidden or neglected by standard accounts of the city. To suggest a move away from an attitude towards urban spaces informed purely by notions of the vertical (and of buildings as singular rather than related entities), is not just a piece of theoretical whimsy, but what seems a timely response to the way in which modern cities are beginning to evolve.

As the operation of dense metropolitan centres is influenced by the establishment of new technological infrastructures, and as many of our cities begin to loosen their belts further into zones of undifferentiated suburban sprawl, urban development is beginning to flatten out, to 'horizontalise'. Although in cinematic terms, it may fit with the new 'megalopolis' that many theorists predict will be the result of this reaching ever-outwards, it is likely that the tall building will have less and less of a role to play in our cities. Originally, as well as being an expression of ambition and optimism, this building type was intended to maximise floorspace. Stacking dense floor plans one on top of another dealt with the problems of both scarcity of land

Below right: An illustration
of Le Corbusier's Plan Obus
'A' for Algiers, 1930, in which
the residential fabric of the
city is conceived as a series
of stacked layers.
Below left: a model of George
Candilis' 1963 scheme for the
arrangement of the centre
of Frankfurt.

and increasing population density, as well as the need to keep people together in one place. With limited communications technology, it was important that someone was just down the corridor, or on the next floor up. But now, in the age of a super-connected global economy, it makes little practical difference if the people we need to be in contact with are just a room, or a whole time-zone away – we can always get their electronic response in seconds. Linked up by the Internet and other digital networks, communities can be as nebulous or as tight-knit as the context demands. So, as both information and relationships are increasingly expressed as webs rather than by physical patterns of architectural (or social) proximity – what Manuel Castells has called 'the space of flows' – it seems that there will be a need to design buildings based on models other than those which stack level upon level.

Whatever happens, the current pace of urbanisation doesn't look set to slow down. Projected figures suggest that by the year 2025, 65 per cent of the world's population will be living in cities. A number of urban doomsayers suggest that a concurrent growth of surburbia as the developmental norm, means there is a risk our established city centres will gradually lose their density, drained of energy and population by the development of what Robert Fishman has dubbed the 'technoburbs' (huge, neo-suburban zones which require no travel into host cities). If we are to reverse this outwards flow, we need to rethink our use of the spaces we have already built for ourselves. In London, Richard Rogers' Urban Task Force is making an already well-documented commitment to a 'rework what we have' approach to urban development, seeking to reinvigorate our cities by rescuing derelict 'brownfield' sites that have been lost to waves of inner-city decay. But the perspective suggested by *City Levels* could be one that pushes this kind of reconfiguration even further. If thinking of our cities in linear terms allows us to identify urban spaces in a different way, might it also open up the possibility of new uses of those spaces? Faced with the prospect of the sprawling megalopolis, it is time to explore innovative solutions.

The challenge of thinking radically about the city's levels was taken up by many visionary architects in the last century. Perhaps most notably, Le Corbusier – with the famous battle-cry 'We must kill the street!' – proposed in projects such as the celebrated Ville Radieuse of 1935 to take the human element of cities into the sky, forcing the linear flows of the traditional street to take a different configuration inside zig-zag residential blocks or stacks, whilst reserving the planes at the bottom of the city for the traffic that connected it to other linear developments and established radio-centric towns. Other grandiloquent plans for applying a radical linear model to the city were put forward by architects such as Corbusian protegé, Georges Candilis. In a 1963 competition to redevelop the centre of Frankfurt, Candilis formulated an audacious scheme, based on the splitting of the different functions of the city and layering them into separate raised levels. Models for Candilis' proposal demonstrate a design for the most extreme built manifestation of the schematic thinking of Modernism, with recognisable landmark buildings overlooking a gridwork of huge platforms that stack one on top of another in what looks like a giant circuit board.

Although there is much to admire in provocative statements about the wholesale reconfiguration of the city, there is a danger in *tabula rasa* ambitions. Time and again, it has been proven that real people in real cities often find it hard to live in the grids of grand diagrammatic planning. There is still a place for audacity in contemporary design, but it seems that projects which seek to integrate existing levels, rather than to impose new city-wide levels may prove to be successful solutions for our space-starved and already complicated cities; sensitive additions to the urban fabric are more useful than unpicking it and starting again. This is not to say that grand programmes are impossible: Wiel Arets' proposal for a dual-level city (see page 54) might look like another piece of Corbusian daring, but his designs for high-density urban living are based on the subtle mixing of suburban residential models with high-rise blocks, rather than an aggressive replacement of one entire urban zone with another. Similarly, S333's application of the 'Megaform' (page 92) is an attempt to alter the isolationist character of the high-rise block by enabling street-level flow to seamlessly move up and around it. There are also other, more metaphorical, ways of embracing the potential of the horizontal urban level. Zaha Hadid's new Science Centre in Wolfsburg, due for completion in May 2001 (page 86) retains views to the town beyond in the design of what is potentially a landscape-dominating building. Its 'permeable' lower half reinvigorates public use of space by allowing people to both see past and walk around the huge feet which lift the main exhibition spaces off the ground. The Wolfsburg project is a particularly dynamic but elegant example of how a singular building can be forced into a productive relationship with the abstract levels that join it to surrounding structures and the wider city.

But *City Levels* does not focus purely on the built manifestations of visions of the city seen from this horizontal perspective. It also examines how people interact with these four linear territories, demonstrating that there is a value in reassessing how we both use and occupy urban space at heights from the top to the bottom of the city. In the era of mobile phones and the new powers of contextual selectivity they have granted us (buses and trains can

A section of an elevated scheme in Bangkok to carry railtracks above the level of the street. Designed to ease traffic in one of the world's most congested cities, service on Bangkok's 'Skytrain' commenced in December 1999. The system comprises 23.5 kilometres of track raised twelve metres above the ground.

The extreme pressure on space in contemporary Tokyo often necessitates the use of roof-level as a functional urban territory.

no longer offer silent anonymity), what will be the fate of the previously most integrated of city levels, the street? Should we try to rescue our public spaces from the threat of social complacency? *City Levels* suggests that it is important to realise that even the seemingly most innocuous city spaces are not valueless, but zones marked by particular patterns of usage and behaviour; witness for example, the edgy territorialism of the pavement-bound office smoker (see page 84). The city street was, until recently, thought of as the realm where urban power was at its weakest. Drop-outs and the homeless sleep there, and even the London tube system throws its drunks out from the bowels the city onto the street at closing time. But the renaissance of urban life over the past twenty years is partly a testament to the fact that this is changing. Many of us are no longer frightened to walk down the streets of downtown Manhattan; and the rise in popularity of *al fresco* eating in Britain means more and more people are able to relax at street level. It seems that for the first time in years, the simple equation of height with power is beginning to be challenged as an absolute rule for our city spaces.

There is also a political element to reorientating our perspective on cities in this way. It is important to ask questions about who gets to access certain city spaces. The phenomenal success of the London Eye (offering many people their first opportunity to gain a sense of the city as an entity, rather than a daily experience limescaled by routine) should prompt us to ask why there are not more vantage points over cities which are free of charge and open to the public. Should there be money spent on ensuring that more buildings, like Caruso St John's new 'permeable' art gallery in Walsall with its hole-punched walls that allow high views of the city back into the building, make a commitment to democratic design? Similarly, why is it that a perspective over the city can be different according to the location of the building from which we see it? Living at height can turn easily turn vantage into disadvantage if the lift that takes you to that city view has been broken for months.

The contemporary city still cannot offer the best of its layers to everyone. To go some way towards changing that, we have to attempt an understanding of the opportunities that the spaces between and below buildings can offer us to see our cities, and ourselves, differently.

Following a series of abortive attempts to renovate it, in 1999 Elliott Bernerd, the chairman of London's South Bank Centre, embarked on a search for an architect to design a new masterplan for the site. Bernerd sought to realise the full cultural and commercial value of one of the most important urban public spaces in Europe, situated as it is on the south bank of the river Thames. One of the perceived problems with the site, is the series of high-level decks which connect its different buildings, but which are now blamed for causing the Centre to feel bleak and difficult to navigate.

Following an ideas competition, Bernerd and his team selected Rick Mather as masterplanner, for his proposal to create a landscaped park on the roof of a new headquarters for the British Film Institute. However, another of the participating architects, Rem Koolhaas, made a strong case for bringing out the best in what the site currently has to offer.

Koolhaas' contention was that the decks themselves do not constitute the main problem, but that their current utilisation means they penalise the site twice, by disconnecting the public both from the ground, and from the bridges which feed into the site. For Koolhaas, by removing one of the buildings (the 'irredeemable' Queen Elizabeth Hall), and replacing it with a

new high-level circulation deck connected to the river level by a large ramp, the upper deck could begin to work as it was originally intended to do: as a balcony overlooking the river.

By transforming the walking platforms from interstitial spaces to event spaces in their own right, Koolhaas aimed to provide the vital link between each of the buildings on the site, and in effect to blur the boundaries between them. The surprising act of overturning existing prejudices against the element of the site currently perceived to be its weakest (in fact, even as the masterplanning competition was taking place, some of the overhead walkways were being demolished), is a gesture which could only come from Koolhaas. But if successful, the scheme would also allow for the celebration of some of the quirkier aspects of the overhead decks, such as the spider-leg stairways leading down to lower levels, and their slightly labyrinthine nature.

Ultimately, this was a subtle intervention rather than a grand architectural 'master strike'; a gentle acknowledgment of the centre's current successes in opposition to fashionable cries that the entire site is an eyesore. It is to be hoped that Koolhaas will be given the opportunity to develop his ideas in one of the building projects that will inevitably be generated by Rick Mather's winning masterplan.

SOUTH BANK CENTRE MASTERPLAN PROPOSAL
REM KOOLHAAS

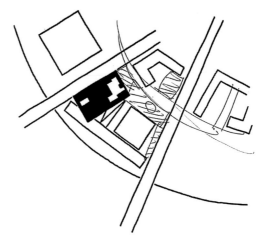

Left: Koolhaas' model illustrating a new two-tier deck area, reached by a large ramp which would bring pedestrians up from river level. The deck is located around a renovated Hayward Gallery, but the Queen Elizabeth Hall has been removed.

Below far left: a first sketch for the masterplan shows the new deck area in black, and the existing riverfront walkway acting as a 'balcony'.

Bottom: the existing buildings on the site are brutally separated from Waterloo bridge, but the staircases between levels suggest some intriguing possibilities within the existing infrastructure.

The highest point

JONATHAN GLANCEY

A ride into the moist skyscape above the South Bank on the London Eye offers a gull's-eye view of the capital's architecture – good, bad and indifferent – which blurs into a great carpet of concrete and brick, glass and stone that stretches out to the hills that frame the Thames estuary. The crowds turned out in force for a occasion similar to the opening of the Eye 217 years ago in Paris, when the Montgolfier brothers flew an exquisitely decorated hot-air balloon carrying a sheep, a duck and a cockerel over the city in the presence of Louis XVI and Marie Antoinette. These animals were sent on their mission for the same reason that dogs were later sent into orbit by the Soviets – to prove that animals (and hence humans) could survive high above the earth. Unlike Laika, the Moscow stray blasted into space aboard Sputnik 2, the Montgolfiers' animals made it back to earth in one piece. Pilatere de Rozier, a science teacher, and the Marquis d'Arlandes, an infantry officer, flew in a Montgolfier balloon three months later. They made a journey over Paris of five and and a half miles and lived to tell the tale. More than that, they came back with a new view of not just the French capital, but of cities in general.

It would be another 120 years before the Wright brothers finally got a heavier-than-air machine off the ground under its own power. Yet the bird's-eye view first described by de Rozier and d'Arlandes stirred a new perception of what a city might become if planned from an aerial perspective. That legacy is clear to anyone who has looked down on Paris from a plane or the top of the Eiffel Tower and been awed by Baron Hausmann's grand, militaristic avenues and the radiating streetscape that emerges star-like from the hub of the Arc de Triomphe. It looks as if some rational god – Blake's Ancient of Days perhaps – has set his compass on the face of Paris. This is urban planning carried out on a Napoleonic scale and with as much tender feeling as resides in the breast of a hovering bird of prey. After the Montgolfiers ... la cité du ciel.

High in the sky, you can't help wanting to redesign what's laid out beneath you. The imperfections of cities like London seem all too apparent from the air, even though the glory of our capital is its mix of serpentine streets, wandering tidal river and lush parks overlaid here and there by sudden bursts of rational eighteenth-century town planning or the grid of later estates and inner suburbs. The great Swiss architect Le Corbusier couldn't help but see things this way. In 1935 he produced a curious book, *Aircraft*, in which he looked down from the great height of an architect's eye and saw cityscapes revealed in all their muddle and vulnerability. He knew, and said, that this view was a revolutionary one. Now we could see what was wrong with cities (the clogged, yet romantic density that holds such appeal to so many of us today). Now we could see how to replan them with surgical precision, to separate cars from pedestrians, workshops from homes, the bourgeoisie from the proletariat. The dangers of this way of thinking about cities are easy to see. As well as gaining a perspective, you may lose one. A colossal city with a rich, miasmic life can become less than an anthill – an artefact rather than a dwelling place. And what worked for a compact site like nineteenth-century Paris does not always work for a modern metropolis.

Above: a view over the River Thames shows how from its central position on the side of the river, the British Airways London Eye can offer viewpoints in all directions, right across the capital. Opposite: at 135 metres high, the London Eye is the capital's fourth-tallest structure, and offers visitors riding in one of its 32 capsules spectacular views of the city. Each 'flight', or full 360° rotation, takes thirty minutes to complete. The wheel's graceful arc is proving a very popular addition to the skyline: in the six months after full operations began in March 2000, over 2 million people came to see London from this new vantage point.

When a city grows so big that it's impossible to see across except from, say, a 443-foot Ferris wheel, it becomes anonymous in key ways. On this scale – the scale of London, Los Angeles or Tokyo today – the imposition of giant grid-irons becomes the stuff of wind-swept avenues and plazas, overscaled buildings, an absence of the small-scale shops, alleys, markets, winding lanes and unexpected moments that make old cities, at their best, such a delight. Instead of people on the move we have traffic flow, instead of homes we have domestic units, instead of small-scale interventions by architects and planners, we have grand schemes that take little account of the people who live in particular areas. This was notably true of the High Victorian city when huge swathes of housing (slums, it's true, for the most part) were scythed through to make way for the triumphal arrival of the railways. Or again, in the the 1950s and 1960s when planners and city engineers, wired up by gung-ho local politicians, drove dual carriageways through the hearts of our urban centres. City plans, drawn up by worthy academics and architects in the middle of the twentieth century, began increasingly to resemble wiring diagrams at one level and air-charts on another. London, according to a plan of 1944, was to be rejigged to make way for no fewer than five circular roads (today's M25 is one, the North-South circular is another). Scale and distance had made the city, in the minds of those responsible for its development, into a featureless map. Looking down from an aerial perspective, the city appeared to be manageable in a scientific and rational way. Now it could be replanned, restructured and, above all – to use a word fashionable in planning circles in the post-war era – zoned. This land would be factories, this bit for 'residential use', this bit for 'retail', and roads would link them together.

It's difficult not to feel omniscient when looking out over a city from the height of the World Trade Center, the Eiffel Tower or the London Eye. It's the sort of view emperors and dictators have always adored and that developers love to show clients. But this high view of cities can be dangerous. This is the same view that bombers of the Luftwaffe's Condor squadrons had of Guernica, that Heinkel and Dornier crews had of London during the Blitz, that USAF and RAF crews had of Dresden. The view, more or less, that Nato pilots had of Belgrade: at the end of the twentieth century, what military pilots really saw was a computer-generated infra-red target, removed as far as technology allowed from the reality of children waiting to go to school or an old dog asleep in a dusty square. Viewed from such a distance, life-filled cities become nothing more than abstract patterns. Ride the London Eye by all means, but remember that the humble worm's-eye view of the city – the view from the alleys, unexpected piazzas and ragamuffin street markets – is just as important as the bird's-eye view of architects, planners, dictators and God.

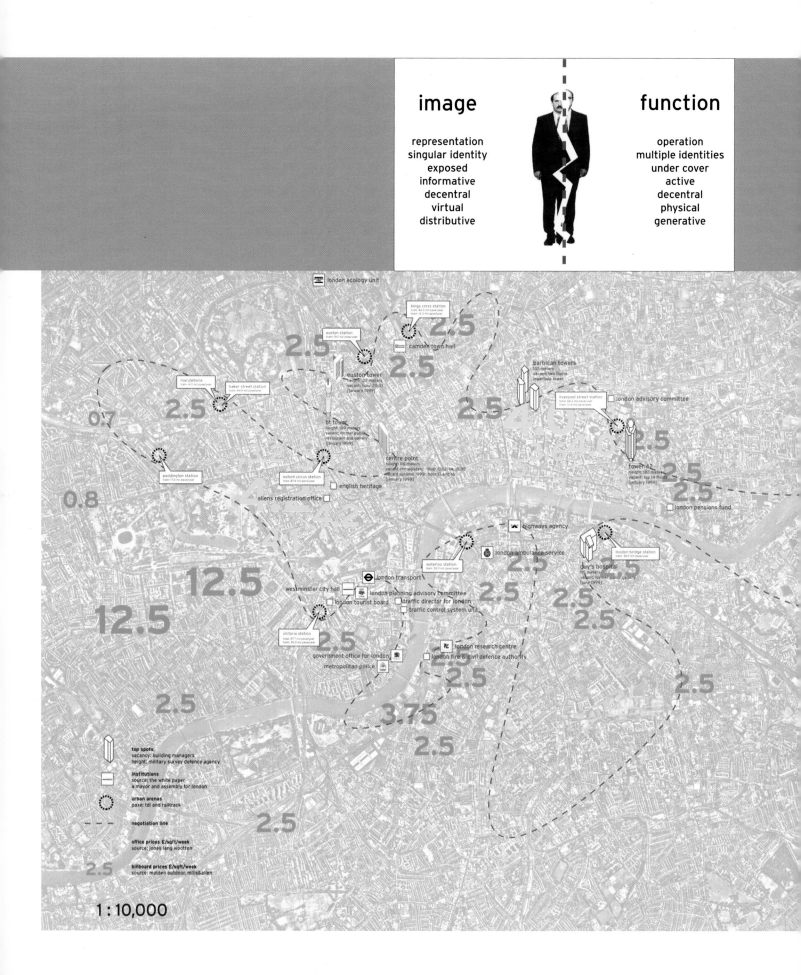

image

representation
singular identity
exposed
informative
decentral
virtual
distributive

function

operation
multiple identities
under cover
active
decentral
physical
generative

london ecology unit

kings cross station
tube 86.0 mil pave/year
train 12.0 mil pave/year

2.5

euston station
train 19.0 mil pave/year

camden town hall

2.5

2.5

marylebone
train 4.0 mil pave/year

baker street station
tube 84.5 mil pave/year

2.5

barbican towers
137 meters
vacant: two floors
lauderdale tower

euston tower
height: 122 meters
vacant; floor 20-33
(january 1999)

liverpool street station
tube 44.0 mil pave/year
train 11.0 mil pave/year

london advisory committee

0.7

2.5

2.5

bt tower
height 189 meters
vacant; former public
restaurant and gallery
(january 1999)

paddington station
train 17.0 mil pave/year

oxford circus station
tube 87.8 mil pave/year

2.5

tower 42
height: 183 meters
vacant: top 14 floors
(january 1999)

centre point
height 116 meters
vacant immediately: floor 10-12, 14, 15,30
vacant autumn 1999; floor 13 and 16
(january 1999)

english heritage

2.5

0.8

aliens registration office

london pensions fund

highways agency

london ambulance service

guy's hospital
111 meters
vacant; former public gallery
(june 1999)

london bridge station
train 36.0 mil pave/year

12.5

waterloo station
train 55.0 mil pave/year

2.5

2.5

12.5

westminster city hall

london transport

london planning advisory committee

london tourist board

traffic director for london

2.5

traffic control system unit

2.5

victoria station
tube 87.1 mil pave/year
train 50.0 mil pave/year

london research centre

2.5

2.5

government office for london

london fire & civil defence authority

metropolitan police

2.5

2.5

3.75

2.5

top spots
vacancy: building managers
height: military survey defence agency

institutions
source: the white paper
a mayor and assembly for london

urban arenas
paxe; tdi and railtrack

— — — **negotiation line**

office prices £/sqft/week
source: jones lang wootton

2.5 **billboard prices £/sqft/week**
source: maiden outdoor, mills&allen

2.5

1 : 10,000

GLA PROJECT OLE SCHEEREN AND HENRIK ROTHE

Above right: Scheeren sports a special mask in order to define the appropriate area for eye-level mayoral communication.
Above left: the job of mayor is split into two distinct roles.
Left: a map of the connections made by the MexT urban negotiation team.
Below: the different levels of mayoral expertise mapped onto the city's building heights.
Bottowm: the available office space in London's seven tallest buildings.

Ole Scheeren is a Rotterdam-based architect working with OMA. A graduate research project at the Architectural Association, conducted together with Henrik Rothe, investigated the possibilities for accommodating the newly-formed Greater London Authority and its mayor, Ken Livingstone. The result is radically different from the Norman Foster-designed building which will eventually house the authority.

Scheeren's goal was to identify the social, territorial and economical value systems which influence the media and physical space of the urban realm. By choosing a system of local government, which manifests itself both in three-dimensional space and equally importantly in media space, he discovered an ideal subject for research. In a series of iterative research steps,

Scheeren worked his way through discoveries and deductions which can only be summarised here in the briefest way:

1. Split Mayor. The roles of the mayor and the governing authority are split into two kinds: the representational role, in which ideas are communicated, policies broadcast and the mayor acts as a statesman for the city; and the operational role, in which policy is implemented and action taken.

2. Zones of expertise. In an extraordinary metaphorical leap, Scheeren and Rothe equated the levels of expertise required for the successful operation as a window cleaner in London (the higher the building, the more professionalised the window cleaner must be), with the levels of mayoral expertise required before and after the election. They equated lower levels in the city with the 'free negotiable' zone: the mayor acting at the most representational level. Higher levels were designated as the 'professional' and 'superprofessional' zones, inaccessible to most people, and equated with the operational role of government.

3. Using these zones of expertise, Scheeren developed the VOCS (Virtual Organisation and Communication System); an information system of government distributed through eye-level media such as cashpoints.

4. Fix-points – representational. Seven designated points at railway

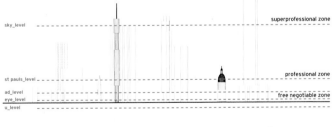

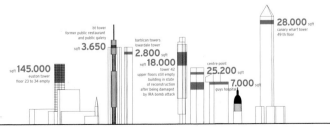

london line display

the london line display
is used as an representation and
interaction device
the MexT projects images of the
london line onto the screen,
londoners have got the opportunity
to interact immediately

travelator accessing the bowl negotiation table

view corridor bowl 01 - barbican tower

top spot 04 barbican towers

the barbican towers are the second
farest top spots of bowl 02

negotiation table

the contact point for londoners
to meet the MexT
the table also invites people
passing by and potentially
the mayor
from the table there is a
view corridor
to the next top spot,
which is euston tower
for bowl 01,
kings cross & st pancras

MexT base station

the base station of bowl 01 is
accommodated in vacant spaces
at barclays bank on euston rd
the offices are utilised by the MexT
as service points, wher all
equipment is stored,
the space also works as resting room
for the MexT

MexT projection room

the london underground maintenance box
provides space for the Mex-projection Team
the existing box will be kept
for that purpose

london institution 01 camden town hall

the building, currently hardly accessable,
will be opened to the public by adding
a new escalator
the new access destabilises the institution
by the possibility of the permanent presence
of the unexpected visitor
the 30 seconds preparation period to access the building
is introduced by use the escalator

key

the MexT meets londoners at the negotiation table
the table is the fix point along the line
the site of the table changes accordingly to events

the MexT base station operates as the studio, where
the MexT prepares the london story
the MexT base station accommodates the tools for the dayly operation

the 'london story' is projected from the MexT projection room,
accommodated in the existing london underground service station,
which is providing electricity

1 : 200

Above right: a continuous strip of advertising hoardings weaves through the city at first-floor level.
Above: The Fix-Point at King's Cross Station, where mayoral messages would be transmitted from a huge hoarding, and an urban amphitheatre would act as a popular meeting point.

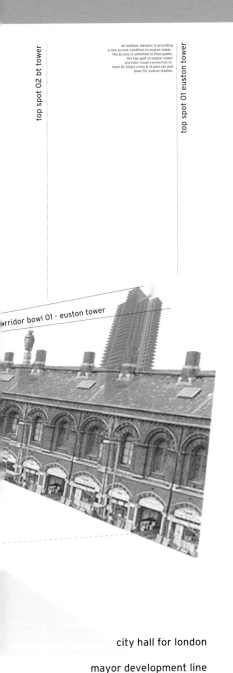

top spot 02 bt tower

top spot 01 euston tower

an outdoor elevator is providing
a new access condition to euston tower.
the access is unlimited to thye public.
the top spot of euston tower
provides visual connection to
bowl 01, king's cross & st pancras and
bowl 02, euston station.

rridor bowl 01 - euston tower

city hall for london

mayor development line
bowl 01
kings cross & st pancras

m ⊖ t

termini in London, excavated to one metre below surface level. Here, Scheeren created urban arenas which could act as public assembly points, or points at which information from the GLA could easily be transmitted to the highest number of people through large information screens (and the commercial revenue from these screens would finance the lease of GLA accommodation).

5. Fix-points – operational. Scheeren discovered that significant amounts of office space are available in London's seven tallest structures. He proposed that GLA offices should be placed in each of these buildings, to accommodate the 'super-professional' operational activities of government which do not require public access.

6. MexT (Mayor Expert Team). Scheeren proposed that a team of 'urban negotiators' would move through the city, establishing lines of relationships and connections between different parts of the city. The lines and trajectories (see main map) would be in constant flux, gradually covering the entire terrain of London. Originally conceived as a continuous strip of advertising weaving through the city, after detailed discussions with a number of potential 'shareholders' in the project (individuals who he managed to persuade to give up their first-floor window space to accommodate a hoarding) Scheeren realised that gaining

planning permission for a weaving advertising hoarding would be impossible. After further research, he calculated that the revenue which could be generated from the Fixpoints at the London stations would be sufficient, and that mayoral communication at this level could be a more fluid proposition.

7. Mayor. Acting at the 'super professional' level, the mayor would move through London between the different governmental locations, mediating and connecting the heterogeneous particles of the system.

8. The split citizen. By integrating the process of government into the daily activity of citizens, the mayoral structure would thus constantly be confronted by the public and private persona of the individual.

Utopian though the project may seem, Scheeren's investigations reveal the surprising extent to which we take for granted our supposedly-democratic processes of government, and also the hierarchical strata of social and political organisation which structure life in the city. At the same time making manifest, and subtly appropriating these structures, Scheeren offers up a model for urban planning which is sure to find a real-life application in the near future.

Below: chart illustrating the world's tallest buildings to date, and those which may follow.
Right: Berthold Lubetkin's Highpoint 1 flats, Highgate, London.
Opposite: Lakeshore Drive, Chicago, designed by Mies van der Rohe.

ON THE ROOF
LAURA HOUSELEY

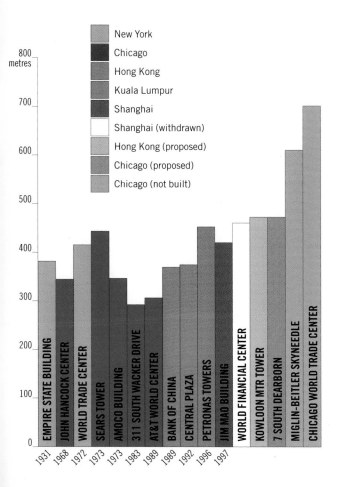

Chart legend:
- New York
- Chicago
- Hong Kong
- Kuala Lumpur
- Shanghai
- Shanghai (withdrawn)
- Hong Kong (proposed)
- Chicago (proposed)
- Chicago (not built)

Y-axis: metres, 0 to 800

Building	Year
EMPIRE STATE BUILDING	1931
JOHN HANCOCK CENTER	1968
WORLD TRADE CENTER	1972
SEARS TOWER	1973
AMOCO BUILDING	1973
311 SOUTH WACKER DRIVE	1983
AT&T WORLD CENTER	1989
BANK OF CHINA	1989
CENTRAL PLAZA	1992
PETRONAS TOWERS	1996
JIM MAO BUILDING	1997
WORLD FINANCIAL CENTER	
KOWLOON MTR TOWER	
7 SOUTH DEARBORN	
MIGLIN-BEITLER SKYNEEDLE	
CHICAGO WORLD TRADE CENTER	

Andy Warhol once said that skyscrapers look like money. He could have gone further and said that inhabiting any of the floors between ground and roof was like loose change compared to the hundred-dollar bill that constitutes life in the penthouse. Whether they function as a home, an office or a bar, the very highest architectural spaces are desired because of their rarity. Rooms with a view – especially a view of the best cityscapes – will always be symbolic of success.

The skyscraper was developed as a response to the high cost of land in urban areas, but the extravagant creations of America's master-builders in the early twentieth century soon gave the high-rise an air of luxury and prestige. Architect Louis Sullivan, in whose native Chicago the nation's first skyscraper, the Home Insurance Building, was erected in 1885, wrote of the new type of buildings: 'The skyscraper is a tool. A magnificent tool for the concentration of population and for the decongestion of soil; a tool of classification, and for interior efficiency; a prodigious force for the improvement of working conditions and a creator of economies; for these reasons it is also a dispenser of richness.'

The period between the end of the First World War and the Wall Street Crash of 1929 was marked by a boom which was mirrored in the changing silhouette of the country's larger cities. Steel framing and the elevator, essential elements for making the skyscraper a viable proposition, had been mastered a generation earlier but were now being used with a new audacity. Thoughts of possible crisis were far from architects' minds as corporate buildings grew ever higher. Van Alan's New York Chrysler building caught the imagination of a nation in the late 1920s, the Rockefeller Center in the 1930s was one of the first of Manhattan's monster monuments to boast roof terraces, and in 1950, Mies van der Rohe's Lakeshore Drive in Chicago was the first residential building to buy into the corporate aesthetic. The Lever House in New York, SOM's contribution to a fast-growing skyline, not only had marble entrance halls and chrome fixtures but a roof terrace that stretched the length of the building. The quality of the services, fixtures and fittings was paramount – a style which has since been slammed for its lack of social and urban responsibility. But America's home-grown buildings of this period remain signposts of a time when the vertical dreams of a generation first secured a strong thread between height and wealth.

A pioneer phase of another kind helped shape similar developments in Britain. The situation was very different, with a lack of both progressive clients and talent combined with the pervasive influence of the Arts and Crafts movement. Modern buildings and ideas from abroad were regarded with suspicion. Nonetheless, the sensibility created at the Bauhaus in Germany did infiltrate British thinking: one of the most acclaimed projects produced by Britain's Modern movement was Berthold Lubetkin's Highpoint 1 flats, built between 1933–5 in North London. The building's penthouse suite embodies much of the Modernist ideal of efficient living: wrap-around terraces, an elevator that opens up straight into the living room, climbing shuttering (a first for residential building in the UK), concealed heating – design elements that expressed the optimism of pre-war Britain. But by the 1950s, there was mounting public concern at the increase of both residential and commercial tall buildings, and the threat posed by

unchecked speculative development. In the wake of the abolition of the general needs subsidy in 1956, the public housing sector's new emphasis on slum clearance only hastened the trend toward constructing higher blocks in order to meet density targets.

Although designed in the 1950s by Chamberlain, Powell and Moya, London's Barbican Centre wasn't built until the early 1970s. The realisation of a long-standing urban ideal, it incorporated cinemas, art galleries, apartments, working spaces – and penthouses. The situation in post-war Britain had offered every opportunity for experimentation, and once again, the penthouse as a design element came into prominence. Its referent remained the socialist ideals of an earlier generation's experiments on the Continent,

particularly the roof terrace of Le Corbusier's Unité d'Habitation in Marseille, which featured a gymnasium, crèche, pool and running track. Le Corbusier's experiments with the utility of high-rise spaces – intended as an antidote to the squalor of the industrial city – were to be repeated the world over.

Ever since the early boom in high-rise building, the penthouse has enjoyed periodic moments of favour. It seems that when a city is cashing in, a renaissance of interest in rooftop bars, casinos and hotel suites follows. As a notional community, the jet set never seem to be that far from their supersonic window seat – the spaces frequented by the rich do much to promote the legend of high-rise luxury. The swimming pool on the roof of the Singapore Intercontinental, Windows on the World at London's Park Lane Hilton, Kenzo Tang's New York Grill restaurant in Tokyo, the Rainbow Room at the Rockerfeller Center, and more recently the Members' Bar at London's Tate Modern – the exoticism of open space high above the city only heightens the divorce of high-level territory from life on the streets. The private roof garden can be seen as the most luxurious use of space at this level.

The penthouse is central to the construction of idealised perspectives of the city. It offers detachment from the reality of urban life, while the distance and elevation can induce sentiments of superiority and power. It is no wonder the skyscraper and architect have enjoyed a long and fruitful love affair: not only does this building type offer a technical challenge and an opportunity to create a self-congratulatory monument, it also compliments the detached perspective of a city most associated with visionary planning.

And at the summit of these monolithic edifices seen in cities around the world there

is often a crowning glory, a final architectural gesture of confidence in the project and the socio-economic circumstances that brought about its realisation.

The culture of the penthouse is one shrouded with familiar iconic imagery – the successful director in his glazed office, the beautiful young couple inhabiting an apartment four times the size of their neighbour's below, or the luxury hotel penthouse suite. A 1980s sit-com springs to mind: set in the Bonaventure Hotel in Los Angeles, *It's a Living* was broadcast from the bulbous slow-revolving restaurant at the top of this cartoon-like structure, designed by John Portman in 1976. Complete with eternal blondes and tanned torsos, the architecture of the Bonaventure, was the perfect venue for a tale of wealth and superiority. Detached and distanced from the host city, the impenetrable nature of the highest points has ensured them an association with privilege. It's the sheer distance from floor to firmament that leaves us all, master-builders included, a little giddy at the thought of life at the top.

'One's body is no longer clasped by the street ...
Nor possessed, whether as player or played, by the
rumble of so many differences. The city's agitation
is momentarily arrested by vision. The gigantic mass
is immobilised before the eyes [and the] ordinary
practitioners of the city live 'down below', below
the thresholds at which visibility begins.' Michel de Certeau

Although recently eclipsed by the London Eye as the capital's favourite vantage point, the hot-air balloon tethered in Vauxhall still quietly takes thousands of sightseers each year into the sky over South London. This symbol of our need to get up above, and possibly away from, the city was chosen by artist Judy Price as the focus for a video piece – *Axis II* – about the notion of perspective and a desire for 'elsewhere'. The split-screen installation juxtaposes continuous footage of the balloon shot from below with footage taken through an aperture in its basket, which looks down onto one of inner-London's most ragged street plans. The balloon, with only an occasional aeroplane flying above it to interrupt the clarity of its form against a postcard-blue sky, seems to represent an embodiment of the calm that we seek, but often do not find, in the environment below. The piece enables us to see the city transformed into diagrams, a view which makes it easier to imagine we can make sense of what we see; as Price says '… what interests me is the paradox of the desire for detachment and the illusion that through an overview we can achieve some unification with the landscape.'

UP AND AWAY
JUDY PRICE

Elevated territories

**KATHERINE SHONFIELD
JULIAN WILLIAMS**

'...the architect: his hand was known
In heaven by many a towered structure high,
Where sceptered angels held their residence
                                    ... how he fell
From heaven, they fabled, thrown by angry Jove
Sheer o'er the crystal battlements: from morn
To noon he fell, from noon to dewy eve
                                ... aught availed him now
To have built in heaven high towers...'
John Milton, *Paradise Lost*, Book 1, Verses 732–49

Three steps to heaven

For John Milton, writing exactly three hundred years before the most vociferous condemnations of the towerblock, heaven could not be depicted other than by 'many a towered structure high'. Satan was once God's favourite angel, and also, we note, the original architect of the high towers. What better way to show the enormity and horror of Satan's sin than to depict him slung out from this crystalline paradise, and falling for a whole day. If it takes a body less than ten seconds to fall from the highest tower on earth, those heavenly towers must have been some height.

What can this fable tell us about our own dreams and desires to inhabit the heaven of a high tower? For us sinners on earth, heaven is the inhabitation of towers, and because we have sinned it must remain a fantasy. We can never achieve it; we will never build as tall as Milton described three centuries ago. So the very act of looking from the earth at a tower echoes the feelings of banished Satan: the desire to get back to the blissful and unachievable state when we lived within. This text explores what is, despite the chequered history of the residential towerblock in the West, a persistent primal fantasy: the three steps back to a lofty heaven of inhabitation.

The first step replicates the desire for heaven of an exiled sinner. Imagine yourself inexorably walking towards a high building, which you can see in its entirety from far away, your head lifted up, dreaming of possession of the tower through inhabitation: it is literally your object of desire from afar; one embodied in a photograph of Lever House, in Manhattan. In step two, you have achieved the site of your desire: you are within a tall building and you look back to earth from on high, and back to the past you have ascended from; as in Denys Lasdun's drawing of Keeling House (one of the first towers to be built in the East End of London) with its view of St Paul's Cathedral. The third step to heaven excludes the earthly, the past and sin entirely: it is desire satisfied. This is the world of high views: from rooms at the top to other exclusive rooms at the top, characterised by the idealised architecture of the corporate boardroom.

Step one: The object of desire

By the end of the nineteenth century, the American city had already seen a vertical extension to rival anything on the planet. Demand for land, especially in New York and Chicago, makes the genesis of the tall building

Lever House, Park
Avenue, New York City,
designed by Gordon
Bunshaft of SOM in 1952
as a corporate headquarters
for Lever Brothers.

a matter for economic logic, rather than mythic desire. Nevertheless, Chicago was the site of some concerted thinking about what might be called the intrinsic qualities of tallness and, especially, the tall building as a thing clad with sensuous beauty. For the architect Louis Sullivan, writing in 1896, tallness is synonymous with an architecture which 'attracts the eye to its location', and which expresses a 'sentiment of largeness and freedom'. The tall building 'reveals to the artist-nature its thrilling aspect. It is the very open organ-tone in its appeal. It must be tall, every inch of it tall ... It must be every inch a proud and soaring thing rising in sheer exultation that from bottom to top, it is a unit without a single dissenting line – that is, it is the new, the unexpected, the eloquent peroration of most bald, most sinister, most forbidden conditions.' Sullivan evokes qualities associated with the phallic male: his tall building is seen from below, it impresses by its power seen from the outside, and it is measured in inches – and, interestingly, it is already a twentieth-century, slightly dystopian version of a heaven to be inhabited, associated with sensuous amoral extremes: 'most sinister, most forbidden'. This is not building-power emanating from economics or use, but emphatically as a vision: an architecture of surface.

Strangely, this at first sight anachronistic vision actually sets the terms for contemporary discussion on the desirability or otherwise of proposals for tall buildings in the City of London. So current public debate of Lord Foster's 'Gherkin' proposal has not questioned the demand for another office block, how the building will affect the public spaces of the street, or whether it will function appropriately. The terms of controversy are exclusively about the building's ability to form a powerful composition with other tall buildings and its surface, i.e. will it be a desirable object seen from outside? The high visibility of tall buildings emerging above their urban surroundings invites a change in the way we experience the city. Their monumental scale in modern cities, where official monuments are conspicuous by their absence, makes a kind of visible register above the intimate spaces of our immediate experience. Whilst these two spatial territories are constantly connected through the up-and-down motion of our vision, it is rare that we can see, let alone experience, them at one and the same time – they are disconnected spaces. On one level, there is our foreground, fully charged with urban activity engaging all our senses – hanging on to our handbags, avoiding filth and danger in our immediate vicinity, checking out doorways and others using the street – on another, the interior with its complex interweavings of spatial intimacy. In our immediate surroundings and above, we might be aware – through sounds, feeling (gusts of wind), the smell of enclosure – of the presence of tall buildings. But our experience of the far distance is dominated only by what our eyes see and our intellect recognises: visible forms silently occupying the sky; we do not smell, hear or feel them in a complex, or confusing, or vibrant way.

This disjunction between the near and far, the immediate and the virtual, has been played out through the depiction of the tall building both before and after its realisation, and has framed the way architects approach thinking about tall forms. The architect's visionary perspective drawing establishes how we might experience the future; the architect's near-perfect photograph

redefines messy immediacy through the replicating of this vision, and offers up a way of seeing that links the dream with the reality which confronts us. It defines how we will see, in a way that reinforces and replays our desires for an imaginary heavenly space beyond our immediate world.

As a space, aloof and otherworldly, Lever House on Park Lane in New York is the quintessential tall office building. It was designed by Gordon Bunshaft of the architects SOM in 1952 as a corporate office for the global giant Lever Brothers, solely to accommodate the company's staff. The building consists of two quite distinct forms: a one-storey podium raised up on columns, and an eighteen-storey slab block above. The slab block is aligned at right angles to the street and appears to float thanks to the recessed curtain-wall glazing at its base above the podium. The design breaks with those of its predecessors, and follows Le Corbusier's call to abandon the street as a corridor lined by high buildings. Whilst the podium addresses the street with a frontage and entrance, the slab above appears to occupy a different and altogether more visionary space. It dislocates itself from its surroundings and from us – the slab stops before reaching the level that we as viewers from outside the building are inhabiting.

In a later and much publicised photograph of Lever House, the viewpoint is again taken at street level, but from the opposite plaza of the subsequent and even more influential Seagram Building by Mies van der Rohe of 1958. The foreground establishes our (fictional) position: framed by the ground-floor arcading of the Seagram building, cut off from the street and other buildings by a large reflecting pool and a flowerbed. The water confuses our sense of distance – the lines of perspective are stopped and distorted by water and the minute scale of its ripples – and our ability to make connections between the zones of the distant and the near is therefore baffled. The building's slab exists in an impossible space – in earthly terms at any rate – beyond the water and the podium, higher than the viewer, offering in terms of the composition an unreachable sense of power, vision and greater privilege. In the foreground of the picture stand three confident figures, a man and two women; the man facing squarely towards Lever House. They are not passers-by, they are tower-viewers: their gaze is carried across the water and upwards towards the sky. Their eyes are led from the real spaces of ground level, up into the air; their desire collapses the distance between themselves and the floating block.

Long shadows of either late afternoon or early morning fall onto the building's façade whilst the lower half is cast in darkness. The broad side elevation of Lever House shifts from relative transparency in the lower shaded section to a shimmering opacity as the sun hits the glass. As the building rises towards the sky, it appears to become more solid and loses a sense of scale: the individual glass panes merge to form a wall that disappears into the distance. At the lower shaded levels, the interior rooms are still just visible. Further up and this tangible connection is lost; the building becomes a miraculous, sheer glistening wall, a crystalline battlement, its interior occupied not by visions of the eye (because you cannot see inside) but of desires generated by the imagination. The people in the foreground look up to a site of powerful possibilities, a realm, like heaven, lying beyond reality.

The Lever House photograph invites us, displaced in the same way as these tower-viewers, to dream about occupying the slab, to be at height, at a level of status.

The game of desire played out between the viewer and the tower is a game where the tower plays hard to get. This goes some way to explain the habitual suppression of the entrance in the residential tower: the building is alluring, but does not give away how to get in. While exigencies of economy might account for the small scale of entrances in residential tower blocks built for the masses, it does not tell us why no reference is made to the way in anywhere on the façade. The façade of Erno Goldfinger's Balfron House is all eyes, a surface of changing windows continually moving and never the same. Built in the 1960s, an era when attractive women were seen and not too often heard, its aesthetic parallels the kind of make-up which blots out the mouth, making it the same colour as the surrounding skin, and dramatically emphasises the eyes. Despite, or because of, the emphatic virility of Louis Sullivan's description of the tower's seductive power, the analogy with the silent female, whose allure must be entirely visual, is almost inevitable.

Step two: Desire acheived (looking back and looking down)
Keeling House is an iconic residential towerblock close to the financial centre of London in the traditionally working-class area of the city, the East End. Short by contemporary standards, it stands just fifteen storeys above ground. Yet it dominates the surrounding landscape, visible in its entirety from afar. Its architect Denys Lasdun's own representation of the view from the interior shows the desire for the tower achieved – the view across to the landscape of a city of the past. On the communal balconies, depicted as a convivial public space on high, people go about their domestic tasks with calm. Height has removed the social sphere from the impure pollution of the city and its traffic: an idealised communal harmony remains.

The block frames a window onto the city beyond and below. In the perspective, the horizon line lies at the same height as the base of the dome of St Paul's cathedral in the distance, so our view is elevated to a far greater height than it would be in reality. The drawing makes use of the 'cut-away', a technical drawing technique which sees beyond walls with fantasy X-ray eyes, cutting away enclosures. Its use within the drawing implies a series of complex vantage points, from upper to lower level. They allow you to look back to where you have come from, both in space and in time. Time past is conveyed in the quaint higgledy-piggledy single line drawing of the city beyond. Space future, when you will have achieved your desire to live on high, is drawn boldly with heavy shading, emphasising the building's robust solidity, in contrast with the past.

In *Alfie*, the 1960s film about a sexual adventurer abroad in Swinging London, the heaven of sexual fulfilment with one of his many 'birds' is synonymous with the protagonist's insinuation into their domestic interiors. The apotheosis of his success is marked by Alfie's penetration of the high-rise flat. The camera shows a smug Michael Caine directly addressing his

Opposite: towerblock in Hoxton, East London. Top: entrance to a high-rise tower in New York. Above: Keeling House, a cluster block in East London designed by Denys Lasdun, was built in 1956 and refurbished in 2000.

Principals: Jesse Reiser
and Nanako Umemoto
Design Team: Jason Payne,
Yama Karim, Nona Yehia,
David Ruy. Assistants:
Wolfgang Gollwitzer, Astrid
Phiber, Matthias Blass

WEST RIVER CORRIDOR PLAN
REISER + UMEMOTO

Since 1998, New York-based architects Reiser + Umemoto have devised infrastructural proposals which would transform much of the riverfront of the island of Manhattan, in a process the architects describe as 'infrastructuralism'. Their proposals for the East Riverfront have been received to great acclaim, and led to their being invited to participate in a competition for the redevelopment of the West side of Manhattan.

Make no mistake, the scale of Reiser + Umemoto's work is vast. Affecting an enormous area around the existing Jacob Javits Convention Center between 28th and 39th Streets and between the banks of the Hudson River on the west to 8th Avenue at the eastern edge, the proposals interweave the needs of local communities into an extended public and private realm.

The various needs of local groups (whether they be residents, shoppers or convention centre users) are, in effect, wrapped around the existing natural and artificial geography of the site, which includes the huge incisions of the local transport infrastructures. In Reiser's words, 'the railyard, Pennsylvania Station, the Lincoln Tunnel, the West Side Highway, and the Hudson River are all realities of this site operating at scales, intensities and speeds not commonly associated with residential use. Yet it is the uniqueness of this condition which sets this neighbourhood and its residents apart from every other in Manhattan. Our proposal takes advantage of these various features, augmenting them in ways which actually produce more occupiable and desirable occupation than was possible with the existing vast, monofunctional structures.'

The extreme variety of levels within this existing infrastructure generates a variety of 'ground levels' within which spaces are developed. As one moves up from pavement level, the space and organisation tends to respond to the larger scales of the institutions already on the site. At water level, a park space runs along the Hudson riverfront from 28th Street to 39th Street, offering amenities for water-based recreation. Above it, an upper tier of green parkland stretches from north to south, and then turns eastwards between 30th and 34th streets, to form a still-elevated link to the city grid. Much of the raised parkland is covered by what Reiser describes as a 'continuous but differentiated spaceframe, partially glazed and partially clad in steel', to create an event space which seems to be both inside and outside. Within it, outdoor sports are possible, as well as stadium-type concerts which need protection from the elements.

Modulations in the surface will create a variety of different, smaller-scale areas, and the project also finds space for a shopping mall close to the large parkland; as well as an extension to the Javits Convention Centre.

audience while at the same time enjoying the ultimate indulgence, having his toes pedicured and then sucked. Alfie the conqueror is shown against a window beyond which is the undifferentiated grey of a London seen from above, sunk in earthly anonymity. By contrast, views from Keeling House and other blocks reveal the view down from the removed heights of paradise attained is stark. Where the view of St Paul's and its environs is safely innocuous, unmediated by the picturesque eye, the rich, chaotic grain of the past, the city's old structures, seems sordid and ramshackle in the distance. Immediately below, the landscape that surrounds the towerblock takes on the clarity and logic of a plan or map; designed as well as seen, literally, from above. So abstract two-dimensional qualities – the geometry of a perfect curve – are favoured over the view from the ground where such order is meaningless. The functional *raison d'etre* is that more sophisticated service access is required by a tall building: for refuse vehicles, oil tankers and fire engines. But in effect, the tower is surrounded by a *cordon sanitaire*, sanitised in its pure forms as much as in what is excluded when it meets the ground. The tower appears to push back the surrounding urban mess, heightening the disjunction between the existing city and the new form. Looking down, the concrete surfaces appear clean, and extend the scale of the tall structure outwards to the boundary with the grimy surrounding buildings.

Height may remove the body from the contamination of the city, but what of getting rid of unwanted matter from the building itself? The act of throwing away now achieves a new and heightened order – ridding the self of unwanted matter becomes a graphic physical act, just like Jove's expulsion of Satan from heaven where he is thrown 'sheer over the crystal battlements'. J G Ballard's futuristic novel *High Rise* concerns an entire city accommodated vertically, whose inhabitants accept as entirely normal the habitual ejection of the unwanted from above, and the consequent trashing of what lies below:

> '…on the 9th floor, a children's party was in full swing. The parents made no attempt to restrain their offspring, in effect urging them to make as much noise as possible. Within half an hour, fuelled by a constant flow of alcohol, the parents took over from their children. Charlotte laughed openly as soft drinks were poured on to the cars below, drenching the windscreens and roofs of the expensive limousines and sports saloons in the front ranks.'

A scene from the 1966 science-fiction film *Fahrenheit 451* directly illustrates this apparently unstoppable instinct in a disturbing and violent way: the fire brigade, charged with burning all existing books as mind-distorting material, raid a multi-storey block. Books hidden in a first-floor flat are thrown out of windows and from balconies onto the paving below. Firemen, congregating below between the building's pilotis, gather up the strewn heaps of books and pile them into a brazier to be reduced to ashes. The scene was filmed in one of the Le Corbusier-inspired slab blocks on the 1955 Alton West Estate at Roehampton in London. The delicacy of the interior furnishings, their bright colours, soft materials and intimate scale, is starkly contrasted with the rough and brutal textures of the exterior: the concrete balcony and pilotis, the rough and dirty tarmac. As if in inevitable hellish opposition with the paradisical perches up on high, the *cordon sanitaire* surrounding the tower becomes a kind of no-man's land, disconnected from the concerns of life above, be it that of an office worker or a towerblock resident. It is a place 'at the bottom', a place where the wastes and pollution of the block naturally end up; and where nowadays, the smokers – the unforgiven sinners of the twenty-first century – meet for a clandestine puff.

The extrapolation of this desire for the expulsion of unwanted elements to the lowest level can be seen in numerous 1960's urban redevelopment projects. Le Corbusier's vision of a rolling landscape delicately overlaid with blocks and sinuous roads on thin columns is transformed. Instead, networks of pedestrian and motorway routes abandon the ground level for the order of higher level; white new concrete strides confidently over the top of crumbling historic forms. Plans for the redevelopment of Piccadilly Circus in London unveiled by the Greater London Council and the City of Westminster in 1968 included a system of segregated pedestrian walkways linking the whole of the West End, from Regent Street to Covent Garden and eventually the City of London, the city's financial centre. Surviving fragments of the City's 'pedways' still hang above the Guildhall, London Wall and the Barbican. Creative visions pushed the idea of abandoning the ground even further. In Sir Peter Hall's play *London 2000*, the hypothetical new town of 'Hamstreet' in Kent has a road system

> '...planned in a series of gigantic one-way loops, (which) passes under and over the pedestrian alleys and paths, and finally converges on a main spine road under the quarter-square mile of pedestrian deck which carries the town centre.'

Hamstreet's houses were to have front doors onto the safe pedestrian network, but below would be another world – of garages, link roads and expressways. The GLC made a virtue out of the Thames floodplain by building a fragment of this dream above the inhospitable marshes at

Opposite: the residential towers of the Barbican complex, London.
Right: elevated walkways, London Wall.

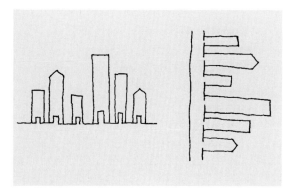

Above: Katherine Shonfield's sketch suggests a different perspective on skyscrapers. Opposite: the view from Space House, Central London, designed by Richard Seifert for the Civil Aviation Authority.

Thamesmead in Bexley. The 1996 film *Beautiful Thing* revisits this vast deck landscape, playing off the 1960s dream with a story of young gay love and liberated social attitudes.

Step three: Desire satisfied – rooms at the top

Seen from outside and from street level, the fantasy of inhabiting the tower is to enter an imaginary space where we might acquire the qualities of the high-rise itself: boldness, monumental dominance, and sheer luxury of surface. But once inside the glamorous object, the experience of the mass of office workers is the open-plan: an undifferentiated sea of desks suspended above the city, excluding light from, and views to, the outside world. In the 1960 film *The Apartment* (set in Manhattan) the life insurance office where Jack Lemmon's hero, C C Baxter works, employs 31,329 people, 'more than the entire population of Nachez, Mississippi'. The special relationship between the single viewer and the tower seen from afar, held within his/her view (our Step one), is dissipated into an interior scape which replicates the anonymity of Manhattan outside. An endless sea of sections and desks is gridded and numbered. The pinnacle of achievement is the key to the executive washroom, a privileged enclosure with exclusive views.

The architecture of the executive suite and boardroom expresses its distinction from the undifferentiated grids below it; it alone is the place which will finally satisfy the individual's desire to attain possession of the tower, by exclusion of all that does not pertain to the celestial realm. And it is from the exclusive suites that harmonious sense is imposed by the building on the modern city surrounding it. New Zealand House, completed in 1963, is a dumpy London version of Lever House's slab and podium tower format. A private terrace for the Commissioner of New Zealand is carved from its enlarged podium; the visitor does not stand on it as at Lever House, but inside it: the frame of building encloses all sides. Views out from the High Commissioner's suite are only possible across, not down from, the terrace, a distance of over ten metres. The outer edge of this terrace is framed by stone-clad canopies to give a series of horizontal slot openings. The view of buildings beyond are edited through these 'windows': the ornate facades of Pall Mall are cut into fragmented strips and masked from the street and their surroundings. External views are drawn in across the terrace, but the building mediates and controls their disorderliness. The edge of the terrace is so far from the office of the High Commissioner that its frame and the view of the city it gives cannot be altered: move nearer or farther from the office window, turn your head up, down, or from side to side, and the view remains the same. The rigorous spatial order of the interior extends its control outwards: it reduces the world to a series of postcard views – still, (street activity is far below) and sensuously framed. The outside is another world, held at arms length for fear of infecting the smooth protocol of the interior fantasy: you literally cannot look down.

By contrast, in the city which Christopher Wren attempted to create in London, following the massive mid-seventeenth century fire, architectural order was understood exclusively at street level. As revealed in his post-fire plan for London, the eye is directed from Wren church to Wren church.

The post-war development of London upset this plan, allowing tall buildings to obscure geographical and architectural inter-relationships formerly comprehensible to the pedestrian. The city of the 1960s and 1970s was dominated by the office buildings of the architect Richard Seifert. His new urban order can be comprehended once again not from the street, but from the heavenly vantage point of his executive suites. The view from the Room at the Top is to other rooms at the top: from Seifert boardroom to Seifert boardroom. This is especially true at night, where the discreet architectural hierarchy of the office block reveals the boardroom distinguished by its lighting from the repetitive forms of the floors below.

The ethereal order is reinstated – literally in the sky – and the rent within the city fabric torn by the construction of the office block is healed. The seclusion of the executive suite became part of a newly idealised interior, wholly different to the industrialised ambience of the horizonless office landscape. Paradoxically, a stylised version of home appears in the places where women's power is completely excluded. The interior architecture of the executive reception and boardroom become inscribed with the visible signs of comfort and relaxation, a decorative setting for a decorative adjunct: the 'girls at the office', the Non-Wife. In a Seifert boardroom at Space House (the headquarters of the Civil Aviation Authority) in Central London, the focus of the interior is all on the sensuous qualities of surface, inviting touch, in sharp distinction to the pre-cast concrete elements of the exterior. Lined with luxurious timber panelling, the boardroom incorporates the built-in storage banished from the architecture of the open-plan ofice. The boardroom is a secret world, a clandestine satisfaction of the desire to possess the object. It exists in opposition to the 'proud and soaring thing rising in sheer exultation from bottom to top … without a single dissenting line'.

The desire for a vantage point: a privatised heaven?

So the dream of the vantage point high above the city is a dream of desire satisfied. But can this desire, as mooted by Denys Lasdun's drawing of families hanging out washing in the sky, ever be public, rather than expressed merely as the personal and private satisfaction of individual power, as in the exclusive interiors of the boardroom? The pressure to construct towers is both constant and consistent, as if we ourselves were Milton's Satan: it seems impossible to conceive of an urban heaven of the future without them. Their inherent exclusivity is questioned by architects who in the past proposed streets in the sky, and who now suggest that public space – sky lobbies – can truly exist high above the city. We persist in thinking of the modern city as a vertical city of towers, like Hong Kong and New York: towers are the most identifiable of signs of a city intent on modernisation. What happens though when you extract yourself from Satan's dream and compare not image but movement?

If you lay the towers on their sides so that they appear not as an elevation, but as a plan to move through, you reveal what is effectively a city of cul-de-sacs – not a modern city at all, but a parochial one. Where you go up you must come down on yourself. The numbers of conduits of movement – i.e.

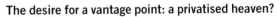

MARTIN LUTHER KING MEMORIAL, WASHINGTON DC, USA
O.C.E.A.N.

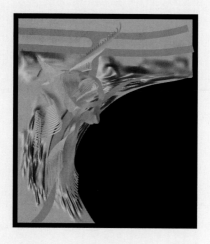

Above: separated strips create paths for walking or marching, their intersections ensuring structural strength.
Left: Plan view of the monument and its location between the lake and the highway.

Project credits
O.C.E.A.N. US: Robert Elfer, Wade Stevens, Kevin Cespedes, Agustus Wendell
O.C.E.A.N. UK: Tom Verebes, Alexander Thompson

O.C.E.A.N., an architecture collective with offices both in the United States and Britain, submitted this entry to a competition for a memorial to Martin Luther King in Washington.

In tune with what it describes as its 'horizontally organised' network structure, O.C.E.A.N. sets out to research the 'vast, smooth space' of contemporary oceanic urbanism, and the Martin Luther King memorial represents one of the possible results.

For O.C.E.A.N., the memory of Martin Luther King rests in the word Movement, in both its senses. King was, of course, leader of the African American Movement in the US, and was highly influential in negotiating improved rights for black Americans after the war. Equally, King's protests came most often in the form of movement – the protest marches which drew so much attention to the cause.

O.C.E.A.N.'s proposed memorial takes the ground plate and lifts it up using a sequence of parallel paths. Each path is imagined to carry one marcher, walking alongside – but separate from – another marcher. These parallel paths lift from the ground to form the built monument, a shape clearly created out of the idea of movement, but whose resulting spaces remain ambiguous. Is it a building or a sculpture? Does it have inside or outside spaces? Would I walk on it? The ambiguous response to such questions is intended. O.C.E.A.N. imagines a series of spaces which encourage contemplation and congregation, but not easy answers.

This ambivalence extends to the placement of the monument within the conservative environment of Washington DC's proposal is to re-route the main West Basin Drive, forcing traffic out of its way to create the maximum impact with the structure, and then lighting each of its curved strips to create a beacon which is glowing, uplifting, and possibly even in motion.

the lifts – are restricted to a few in even the most luxurious of tall buildings. Lateral movement is of course constrained by the edges of the building itself: disembodied glances through windows are the only connections you get; and the experience of movement in a lift is clearly constricted. Although it may be silent and unfriendly, it is the antithesis of the anonymity of a city where public space is based on a fine interconnection of streets, where an almost infinite number of lateral interconnections are possible, and where your movement is restricted only by the impassability of a given thoroughfare. The entry to this vertical cul-de-sac is inevitably through some kind of gate where movement is inhibited, and which becomes a point of control and observation.

Each time a developer tries to assert that they are making public space at high level, we, the public, will pay a price – literally – either now or in the future. The spectacular view from the escalator and at the top of the Pompidou centre in Paris was intended to be free of charge, but by the simple expedient of a ticket booth restricting the entrance, this space becomes exclusive and selective to those willing to pay the fee to the gallery. Planning permission for an exclusive development and restaurant at the Oxo tower, a prominent feature of the South Bank of London's River Thames, was dependent on space given over to the public at high level. In the less-vaunted world of mundane reality, this means running the gauntlet of a doorman, a lift full of elegantly dressed diners and the restaurant itself – scarcely a fun visit for an ordinary South London family wanting to enjoy the amenities of their city. The pretence of a public vantage point in an urban building is revealed in the term 'sky lobby' itself. For those latter-day Satans, it is merely a stepping stone to the posession of the sky itself – and you can be certain St Peter will be there to control who can and who cannot enter that exclusive heaven.

One of the celebrated features of the Pompidou Centre is the views it offers over Paris.

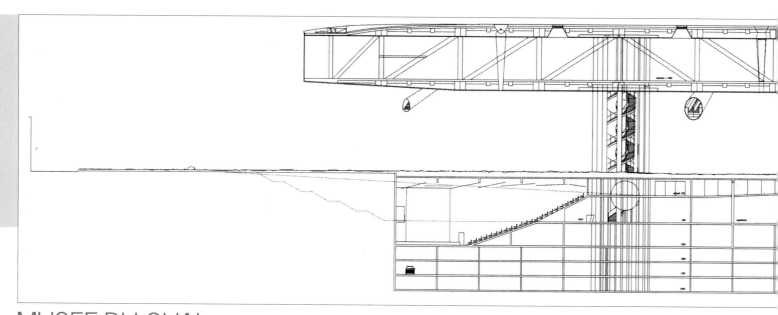

MUSEE DU QUAI BRANLY
RUDY RICIOTTI & PIERRE LOMBARD

Opposite, from top left:
montage pictures illustrating
underground spaces lit by
'fissures' of light; ramp up
to ground level; escalators
in the overhead platform.
Main drawing and overleaf: the
platform stands on three huge
legs, whose hollow interiors
also hide circulation spaces.
Left: aerial view of the site
and its riverside location.

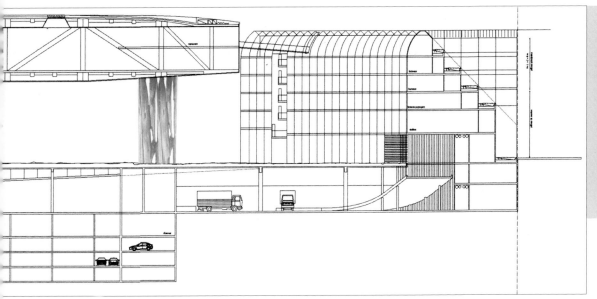

The competition for the Museum of Arts and Civilisations (MAC) on the bank of the River Seine in Paris – the first 'grand projet' of the twentieth-first century – was won by Jean Nouvel. But of all the entries included in the final shortlist (a luminous crowd which included Eisenman, Foster, Piano, MVRDV, de Pontzamparc and Future Systems), perhaps the most intriguing was the one from the French architect Rudy Ricciotti.

Ricciotti is regarded as something of a star architect in France, but his built work is little-known elsewhere. His completed projects include a 5,000-seater sports stadium at Vitrolles and the new Philharmonic Concert Hall at Potsdam. May 2001 sees the completion of Ricciotti's National Centre for Choreography

in Aix-en-Provence, a structure whose walls are built entirely from glass panels, protecting its users from the harsh Provencal sun by employing a simple manually-operated system of boat sails.

Ricciotti treats every project as an experiment in which to kick against the system, and he is not frightened to submit himself to creative risks. This spirit of risk-taking clearly drove Ricciotti's entry to the Quai Branly competition, and given the size of the prize at stake (a 1 billion FF construction budget), one has to admire his courage. In response to a brief which he finds troubling, the architect does nothing short of fracturing the museum's programme into two distinct locations, one underground, and the other lifted off the ground into a huge platform which

stands on three legs. The whole structure sandwiches an enormous garden which occupies the entire ground level.

Rumour has it that Ricciotti's plan was thrown out because its underground levels did not conform to safety regulations, but there has to be a suspicion that the project asked too many uncomfortable questions about the nature of the museum for the taste of the jury. As Ricciotti says, 'the question that really needs answering is: which museum are we talking about? About the one full of colonial trophies, or the one for the twenty-first century? About a museum for every century, or a museum for a guilty twentieth century? This museum cannot be unified, continuous or integrated with the sense that it has all the answers.'

Ricciotti's gambit is to place half of the museum underground, with exhibition rooms situated in a series of 'fissures' through which other possibilities can be glimpsed. Above this, an impressive 16 metres overhead, the exhibition spaces continue in a vast (140 × 60m) platform filled with naturally-lit rooms and giving the feeling of floating over Paris. Between the two exhibition spaces, Ricciotti imagines a garden occupying the full 18,000m^2 site, inhabited by rural plants. By reclaiming the ground and offering it up as a public space celebrating the non-colonial, the non-urban, Ricciotti transforms the museum into a highly self-conscious structure forming an imposing presence around some of the simple pleasures of the natural world.

'The city presents an enigma to the citizen, which is held in place by the principal functionalism of its architecture. In the windows of a towerblock, in the empty lots of a multi-storey car park, in the floodlit pointlessness of an empty tennis court on the roof on an office building there is a sense of mystery – a question without a plausible answer – which compounds the intense romanticism of the urban experience.' Michael Bracewell

MOVING UP
JES FERNIE

The first thing I did when I moved into my flat on the top floor of a twelve-storey building was rip up all the carpets and chuck them off the balcony – the sound of dead weight meeting the ground at high speed reverberated across the street; a kind of echoing thwack that prompted fleeting nightmares of squashed children. Revealed by the removal of the carpet, in the centre of the concrete floor of my living room, there was a curious patch of hastily-applied plaster. I thought nothing of it until the person who owned the flat before me came round a few weeks later (he misses the view) and asked if I had noticed the plaster bit in the middle of the floor. It turned out that when he'd moved in, seventeen years previously, he had discovered a hole leading right through to the downstairs neighbours' bedroom. It was then that I fully registered the layered nature of the space I was living in. I imagined an entire block of inhabitants drilling holes in their floors hoping to catch the peep show of their dreams, seeing nothing but another body lying flat on the floor staring at another body lying flat on the floor staring at another body lying flat on the floor, *ad infinitum*. It was like discovering a towerblock equivalent of Borges' *Library of Babel*.

The English don't like the idea of living in towerblocks; it goes against our traditions and collective instinct for privacy and possessive individualism. Compared to our counterparts on the Continent, a larger chunk of our social status is attached to the ownership of a plot of land which can be defined, hoarded and labelled as something that belongs to us. Living in a towerblock undermines the sense of secure 'grounding' which has in this country become synonymous with ownership; instead, tower dwellers are offered the more ephemeral idea that rather than living on a piece of land, they are inhabiting a space.

At the end of the process of buying my flat, I went to see my solicitor in order to 'exchange'. During our meeting, she read out reams of words which drifted off somewhere between my head and the window, but I did catch her statement that I was '…making the purchase of the flat on floors nine and ten of said block.' I corrected her with, 'No, sorry, actually it's not floors nine and ten, it's eleven and twelve.' But despite continued protests, the solicitor persisted with, 'No, you're buying floors nine and ten.' It took months (twelve, I think) to receive a paper from the council certifying that I had in fact bought the top-floor flat and not the one beneath. I had toyed with the idea of moving into the top-floor and chucking the people downstairs out on the grounds that I owned their flat, but in the end it seemed rather churlish to be arguing over which floor I was on. After all, when you look at a towerblock from the outside, its constituent parts all look the same; there is very little to display the individuality of the people who inhabit it.

Outsiders often assume that the depersonalised look of blocks must in some way reflect on the condition of the people who live inside: a faceless morass of sad and desolate characters who are to be either feared or pitied. But when you actually enter the space of one of the 'cells' that make up these buildings, any sense of uniformity and isolation is immediately inverted. You look out at the view and feel like you are the centre of the universe; you look down on the world and it appears to be yours for the taking. From my balcony I can see St Paul's Cathedral, the Millennium Wheel, towerblocks by Lasdun, Goldfinger and Lubetkin, Kay's City Sauna Emporium at the end of the road, TV aerials, the Millennium Dome, kids playing football, kids abusing other kids, cars, buses, women pushing prams, the Virgin helicopter on top of the Royal London Hospital, trees, sky (lots of sky), buildings being built, buildings being neglected, fireworks, sky storms, aeroplanes, gas towers (exhaling and inhaling through the day), washing, clouds, dogs shitting and pigeons courting. And of course, trains; they thread together the elements of this scenic smorgasbord, weaving their way through the static blocks of the city, a visual and audible beat

which we might once have been able to set our watches by. All this from the balcony. Even when I retire to bed, I am presented with an exquisite, uninterrupted view of the Lloyds building – sex and architecture. Fellow towerblock dwellers come to my flat and scour the view for their buildings. We draw notional pathways across the city which join our homes, an imaginary set of lines suspended above the tangled web of buildings and lives down below that somehow feel like they belong only to us. It is a pleasing conceit which perhaps comes from the satisfaction of being able to locate yourself in a landscape.

All buildings have rhythms, but the rhythms of a towerblock are made explicit by the sheer density of people living in it. I can tell the time of day by the movement of neighbours walking past my front door, by the smell of cooking drifting in through the windows (normally a mixture of curry and boiled vegetables), the sound of rubbish being deposited into the rubbish chute, and by the soft hum of the lift as it collects and deposits passengers. These rhythms are a constant reminder that there is space between me and the ground.

Having lived in my block for some time, the one thing I'm still not used to is the complicated manoeuvre embodied in the sharing of that small bit of moving space called the lift. My front door leads straight out onto an exterior walkway with incredible views of north London; six footsteps later I am at the lift. Inside the lift I am still in public space, but it is enclosed and in motion, slicing slowly down through the layers of my neighbours' flats, through other peoples' lives. Chat about the weather, stare at the back of someone's neck, moan about the state of the lift, think about how romantic it is that someone has written 'sex' (instead of 'fuck') on the ceiling, talk about holiday plans. Then the doors open and I am at ground level, once again in outdoor public space. So every day I make a short journey from private space, through open public space, then restricted public space, to outdoor ground-level space: a routine but still strange form of space travel.

I met a young girl and her mother in the lift soon after I had moved in. She spent the journey staring at me so hard that I found it difficult to ignore her; I smiled and said 'I'm really tall, aren't I?' (I'm 6ft 2"). The girl's mouth snapped shut and she looked towards her mother for salvation. Ever since then the girl greets me with 'You're that tall woman from the lift'. I like the idea of being a nomad giant, weaving my way up and down peoples' lives, occasionally being identified by fellow inhabitants. But the identity of block dwellers need not be primarily based on personal characteristics. ▶

Like the characters in J G Ballard's novel *High Rise*, people in my block are often identified purely by the floor they live on. A neighbour on my floor says, 'It's nice up here, nice and quiet. Not like the fifth floor … all them blacks … never used to be like that'. Instead of segregated, ground-based neighbourhoods where clusters of houses are characterised by specific ethnic (and/or class) traits, my block demonstrates a system of layered segregation in which ethnic distribution is defined vertically rather than horizontally.

Thatcher's 'Right to Buy' campaign of the 1980s and the exploding property market of the 1990s created the conditions for a small minority of first-time buyers to move into ex-council flats in towerblocks, spaces which are still considered undesirable by most people as places to live. The urban professionals who are buying these flats are members of a very specific demographic group: white, middle-class, aged from 25–35, child-free, generally employed in the fields of media, art or architecture. Being part of this group, I am able to see the radically different take we have on living in these blocks, compared to the long-established residents. In their eyes, we are just passers-by. Many of my neighbours have lived in my building since 1958 when the block was built. I don't have much money, but am likely to make

more in the future, and will eventually move on and out. The man I bought my flat from (he is a white, middle-class professional) was leaving because he wanted to start a family, 'This is no place to bring up kids'. There is a couple up the corridor who live in a small two-bedroom flat with four children. Living here isn't a lifestyle choice for them.

Depending on your situation or your frame of mind, living up high can create a whole set of oppositional experiences – characterised by verticality versus horizontality, empowerment versus alienation, uniqueness versus uniformity – that give rise to an unsettling kind of love-hate ambivalence towards the place where you live. I've been here for a year now and there are times when I look down at the nice, neat, clean terraces below me with a sense of envy, yearning for the day when I no longer have to negotiate the lives of my neighbours to such a large degree; and other days when I can't bear the idea of ever leaving the place. I recently found a perfect representation of this state of mind in an exhibition of the work of artist Felix Gonzalez-Torres. In one room, two large piles of stacked paper were placed on the gallery floor. Written in the middle of each piece of paper, in very small script, was:

Somewhere better than this place
Nowhere better than this place

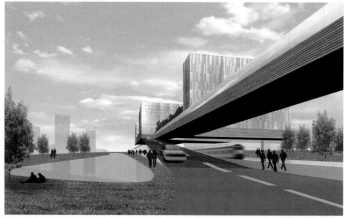

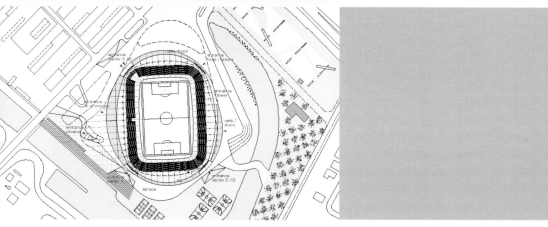

TWO-TIER STADIUM
WIEL ARETS

As Dean of the Berlage Institute in Amsterdam, Wiel Arets has an important position within Dutch architecture. His inclusion among the ten architects invited to submit a proposal for the extension to MoMA New York confirmed Arets' status as one of the best-respected architects of his generation. But Arets' plan for a new stadium in the Dutch town of Groningen is inspired by a modest architectural precedent – the amphitheatre in Lucca, an elliptical marketplace built in the same shape as the building which stood on the site until the sixteenth century. Today, the marketplace has developed two rings of buildings around it, each a mix of housing and retail space.

Taking note of the fact that contemporary cities face an increasing demand for cultural events, Arets has created a sports stadium for Groningen with a number of other attractions included in the mix. As well as a cinema, shops and housing, Arets' masterstroke is to create a playing pitch which can be raised by pistons to the level of the roof, leaving a huge concert hall in its place. The playing surface itself, meanwhile, becomes an open space for residents of apartments in the upper levels of the building complex. Creating a multi-use venue of this size is crucial to the economic success of the project. Traditional sports stadia are often limited to as few as thirty days of commercially-viable playing days per year (the number of home games played by a football team for instance). By creating a grass roof, Arets opens up the real possibility of tripling the income of the venue. Moreover, by mixing residential with commercial use, he hopes successfully to overcome the urban dead zone normally created by large stadia. Like the plaza at Lucca, the stadium also has two rings of seats around it; should it not be needed, the upper ring of seating can be screened off by curtains from the playing field or the stage.

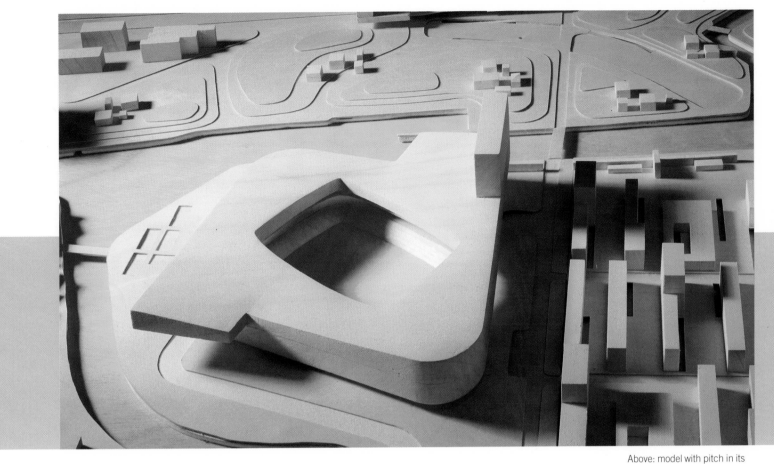

Above: model with pitch in its lowered position; the tower on the upper right of the stadium contains housing.
Below: pistons raise and lower the playing pitch to create a park on the roof with a concert venue underneath.

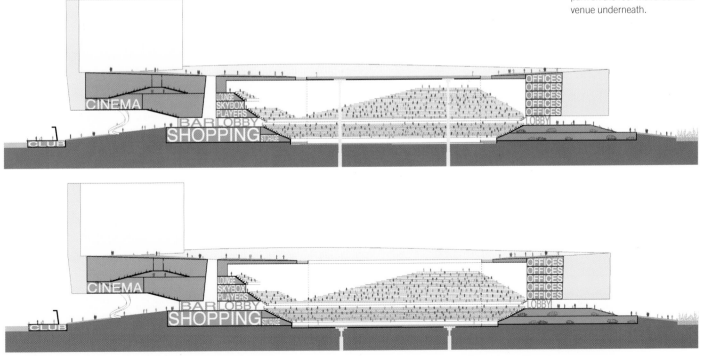

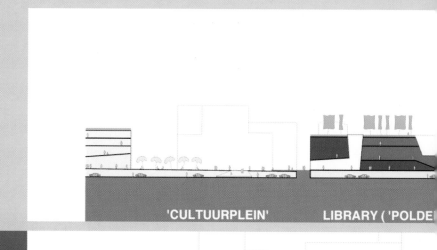

'CULTUURPLEIN'   LIBRARY ('POLDE

RECREATIONAL PARK

TWO-TIER CITY
WIEL ARETS

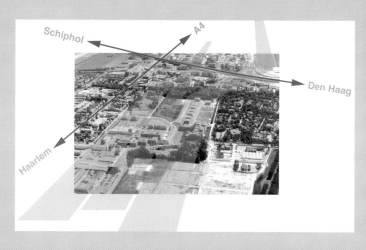

Architects have been attempting to link cities using high-level walkways and skyways for many years. Candilis, Josic and Woods' 1963 project for the centre of Frankfurt, for example, was never built, but another project in the centre of Minneapolis has seen the construction of the city's famous network of air-conditioned high-level skyways connecting 62 different buildings over eight kilometres in length. Minneapolis, however, with its extremes of temperature, is probably one of the few examples of high-level urban planning that has proven popular. It may be surprising, then, that Wiel Arets is now proposing an entire two-tier city which deploys the tactic of a landscaped level, 18 metres above the street.

Located a few kilometres from Schippol Airport, the new city centre for Hoofddorp proposed by Arets will be located at the heart of the Randstad – the über-city which links Amsterdam,

Rotterdam, Utrecht and The Hague, and much of which is built on land known as the Haalemmermeerpolder, reclaimed from the sea 150 years ago. Arets hopes that it will become an influential gateway to the rest of the world for residents of the Randstad, and an important stopping-off point for visitors from elsewhere.

The strategic importance of Hoofddorp's location, however, and the need for high density housing that goes along with that, is only one reason for Arets' twin-level model. Hoofddorp aims to generate differentiated housing typologies and public programmes so as to turn the city into a genuine centre for the entire region. According to Arets, the means of achieving such differentiation is to provide two housing models simultaneously: Hoofddorp aims to combine the cosmopolitan high-rise apartment accommodation generally found in city centres, with the suburban

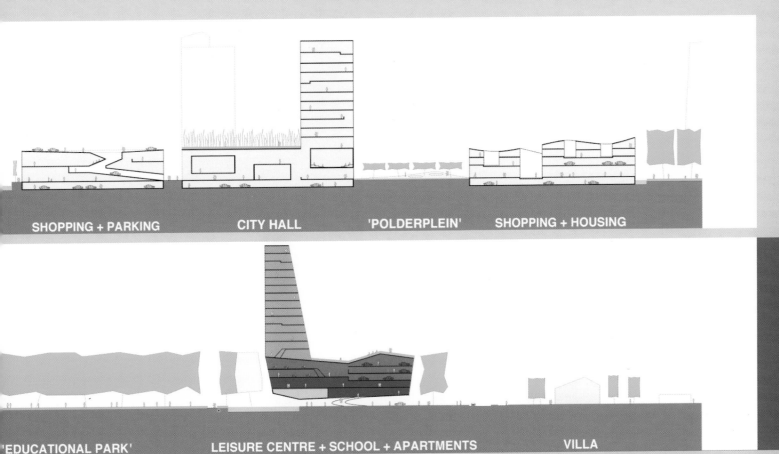

SHOPPING + PARKING CITY HALL 'POLDERPLEIN' SHOPPING + HOUSING

'EDUCATIONAL PARK' LEISURE CENTRE + SCHOOL + APARTMENTS VILLA

model of the single-family-home-with-garden. It does this by placing the suburban gardens on top of leisure and shopping facilities, eighteen metres above ground.

In a recent issue of *Detail* magazine, Arets explained his idea: 'We believe the programme we are proposing for Hoofddorp should be a hybrid one, in which we want to introduce as much housing into the city as possible. The greatest problem in such cases is usually that there is no satisfactory outdoor realm. We want to offer housing with external spaces large enough to allow play and enjoy other activities. In Hoofddorp, we are trying to build a new urban centre. There, of course, the main level is the public realm. Beneath this is a folded structure that forms a second public level – not just a place to park cars, but a place that is landscaped as well. Above this, we have six storeys with commercial uses, dwellings,

a library and a fitness studio. On top of this plinth structure is a further planted level, which is semi-public; in other words, accessible only to residents of the hybrid building. In Hoofddorp, we have provided scope at the top to build 50–60 expensive villas with their own spacious gardens. There is also scope for apartment complexes.'

Arets' plan is materially different from the centre of Minneapolis (and from other proposals for high-level walking cities of the 1960s) for several reasons. Most importantly, each individual building is not linked by a high-level walkway. On the contrary, the second tier of open space in Arets' project is characterised as 'semi-public space', accessible only to residents or users of the building on which it is located. Secondly, Arets' high-level tiers are designated for particular usage, unlike many of the post-Corbusian projects which created heroic

open space without offering any programme to encourage its adoption as part of a local social context. The challenge for Arets is to avoid the expedient solution of a series of high-level private spaces; a perpetuation of an old set of values, where the wealthy few are granted access to their high-level penthouses, while the underclass are, literally, relegated to life at ground level. The correct mix of housing typologies, of domestic and retail space, and of public and private space will be crucial to the success of Arets' proposal.

IZTACALCO PROJECT AT-103

AT-103 was founded by Mexican architects Francisco Pardo and Julio Amezcua in 1999. Its intention is to investigate and create new techniques for architecture in the contemporary city, particularly in Mexico City.

The partnership's initial area of study is the Iztacalco area of the city, where the Avenue Rio Churubusco forms an important traffic artery. The buildings by the roadside are generally occupied by low-income housing with minimal retail services and absolutely no public spaces. Because of the high volume of traffic and poor management of its flow, the effect is to suppress much of the pedestrian traffic in the area.

AT-103's proposal is to restore vitality to the area and transform its character by creating new layers to make an urban village. The proposal is for a three-band circulation plan which consists of an elevated highway with a roof garden, and another layer for mixed use. A tram system at ground level would run along the entire length of the project, with station access via escalators to the mixed-use and residential levels as well as the existing subway system below. The mixed-use level would carry pedestrians along moving walkways to commercial plazas with clinics, schools, offices and supermarkets. The circulation level, on the other hand, would offer only three entry points along its 3-kilometre length, to ensure the rapid transit of cross-town traffic with the minimum of disruption. Above this, on the third level, the roof garden would provide a park and recreational area for the residents of a series of apartment towers spread across the site.

For Pardo and Amezcua, the project would amount to a simple means of reinvigorating a depressed area: 'The re-envisioning of the area is most strongly expressed in the vertical gesture of the apartment towers. On the local level, the project aims to reanimate and enliven the Avenue by the superimposition of the apartment towers and bands of circulation above the existing infrastructures. On the metropolitan level, the project intends to alter the continuous horizontal profile of the city with strong vertical planes that rise up above the suburban sprawl as harbingers of a new artificial landscape'.

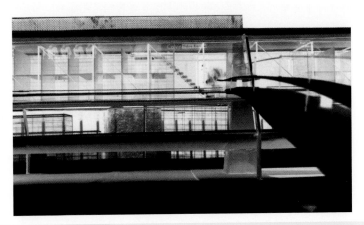

There is much to miss in cities. Boredom, stress or merely the dulling effect of daily routine can mean that we don't take notice of familiar streets and their numberless architectural details: weather vanes, clocks, signage, statues, the texture of a particular wall. Graphic designer Ken Garland has made a point of consciously looking at the city – particularly the level occupied by the very tops of buildings – for years. Garland says this practice is merely an extension of a life-long habit; that he has 'been looking up since I was a boy'.

Garland has always photographed the things he sees above the street, but fifteen years ago, he began to systematise his methods. He now tries to have a camera with him both on everyday journeys around his home city of London (often going back if he is unable to take a picture) and on the trips he makes all over the world. The huge collection of urban fragments he has amassed ranges from the spires of a fairytale castle in Quebec to two statues in Berlin, crying black tears over faces turned green by oxidisation.

Although Garland regards his habit of always looking up as an enthusiasm rather than a rigorous mission, he has tried to adopt a consistent methodology for recording images. Photographing only what can be seen from the pavement, he takes at least two pictures: one of the detail itself, and one of the street or context in which he found it. As a graphic designer, Garland's interest in the city is as much visual as it is sociological (his work provides a means of formalising what he sees), but he emphasises that people can get a lot out of applying the 'look up' rule. Walking into a lamppost is a lesser danger than failing to see at least some of the rich complexity of urban life. Images (from top): Quebec; Dublin; Charing Cross Road, London; Vancouver.

LOOK UP
KEN GARLAND

TWO CITIES
CHEN ZHEN

These strips of images show two contrasting views of the same place at the same time, one seen from the elevated road that cuts through the centre of Shanghai, the other from below it. The view across the city from the road is one of an antiseptic city of grey concrete and glass towers that enthusiastically embrace Western architectural ideals – this is a city racing towards the future. The high-rise template makes this slice of the urban landscape look like a version of globalised Anywhere, with a skyline which is indistinguishable from those of hundreds of other modern cities.

In the tangle of old Shanghai below the roadway, it is a very different story. At the bottom of the city, there are traditional low-level houses and streets full of people going about their daily lives. The bold indications of a specific culture – as well as signs that things may soon change – are everywhere among the colours,

smells and sounds of one of the most vibrant cities in Asia.

Now resident in Paris, Chinese artist, Chen Zhen returned to his home town of Shanghai for the first time in eight years in 1993. This trip was the starting point of a new project to conduct a form of continuous social survey, one which re-assesses the artist's responses to his rapidly-changing native city each time he visits, for the rest of his life. As demonstrated by the long projects he takes on, Chen Zhen sees his work and his life as different aspects of the same creative process.

One of Chen Zhen's long-term projects is to become a doctor. According to traditional Chinese wisdom, an old patient can become a good doctor without having studied medicine; Chen Zhen has been a patient for the best part of twenty years.

The Shanghai project centres on the artist as urbanist. The city is busy trying to catch up with the West, and displays signs of exaggerated acceleration familiar from other Asian centres, where skyscrapers can often be built in a month. Chen Zhen describes Shanghai as 'a big laboratory, because it is a city of immigrants', a place where people live 'as if they were on another continent, separated from the rest of China.'

A city teeming with the complex signs of cultural dualism demands a multi-disciplinary approach to do it justice, so Chen Zhen is using a range of resources, from photography and video to writing and the Internet, to record a variety of encounters and impressions.

The ambition of the Shanghai project is to map the constant developments of a city that is on the move, but which doesn't know where it is going: 'There is no sign of a long-term strategy. That's what's so extraordinary about all the Asian capitals. Total chaos.'

The street

The street is a nomadic place, a transit camp between two thresholds. One connects interior space (both public and private) to the city's exterior connective circuitry; and the other allows movement from this pedestrian zone to the more rapid urban microclimate of vehicular movement – what the street gives us access to appears to be more important than its own often pronounced banality, chaos and unruliness. It is this second threshold that introduces another, experiential kind of exit from the street on the horizontal level of buses, cars, bicycles and motorbikes, trams or boats; down to the subterranean subway, or ascending to an airport departure lounge. The first threshold is long fabled as representing a means of retreat, as well as a communal portal to trade, work, culture and domesticity; but it is also a place of entry before transit or ascent by lift or stair to a higher point of visual reference. But why do we rush for cover from the street?

The street lacks the elevated perspectives offered by tall buildings, but it is in its own right both a real and mythical territory of vantage, as well as a territory which acts as a speculative continuum of cultural, commercial and trading interests. The street is a necessary destination too, if one wishes to understand the contradictions of urban space as a territory marked by both presence and absence. This double-boundaried context that people in cities move through numerous times a day exists on no other level of the city than the street. Historically, it is the place we wanted to escape to, as well as from, a place of self-expression and freedom from domestic ties. Being 'streetwise'

INSIDE NO BUILDING, PUBLIC OR PRIVATE, ON ANY LEVEL, BUT IN THE STREET, DID I: SELL 'FIGHT RACISM', 'FIGHT IMPERIALISM' means the possession of a certain independence, of understanding the ways of modern urban life in order to experience a sense of connection and identification, as well as for gain. In James Joyce's *Ulysses*, Stephen Dedalus insists that tapping the potential of the city – and by implication, the source of life – isn't possible through official, historical sources, but by being aware of 'the shout in the street'; that is, by perceiving the value and nature of individual human energy, the city as a community of people, as well as a landscape.

Overall, since the nineteenth century, the city has been seen as the ultimate location of modernity, social life and revolutionary change. Within its wider fabric, the street is the focus of urban experience, an amorphous, interactive space where unassimilated otherness is most likely to be politically contained and tracked, and at the same time, most palpably perceivable as a reality of life. It is also a protean place in which migration, change and conflict is inevitable; a place of itinerant occupation characterised by a fluctuating language of forms, façades, surfaces and gestures; a place where communal and individual realities mingle, are submerged, flirt, gaze desirously (even for a split second), and fight each other off. Demonstrations *en masse* are the street's natural theatre. During the day, for the solitary walker the street is also a place of intense levelling and heightening of thoughts; and one that, often as much as private spaces, the unconscious frequently unwinds as an arena of expression and decision-making during your sleep.

So what really does happen to you when you tune into the street, as opposed to when you are logged onto the Net inside the more heavily-invested microclimates of many modern buildings; or in your car on the road (which has its own exclusive spatial mythology, extending from Wim Wenders to Jack Kerouac, David Lynch and *Miami Vice* – and all other cop

Opposite: porticoed canalside routes, Venice.
Right: the Lyon Airport Station, France, designed by Spanish architect, Santiago Calatrava.

movies peddling plots full of dramatic and banal street surveillance)? Do you interact conventionally but also in a very specifically open way in this funny, itinerant, levelling and heightening walking place, I'm curious to know? Is your willingness to take part in the *passagiata* stronger away from your daily streets?

Relatively free in the twenty-first century from the scrutiny of poetry or literary mythology – although not yet politics – the street becomes a lacuna, an empty space for something new. In Paris in the 1960s, the Situationists mythologised the city, creating 'drift' travelogues that linked streets and areas in new ways, creating a literary, sub-cultural dialogue about their observations that countered the official histories of tourism or urbanism with an open, contingent and revelatory flow of consciousness. The street is still a medium as well as a place of occupation, and as such, both needs and spurns architecture and design, whose impulses are paradoxically to both contain its energy as well as mirror its life. The spatial identity of the open street, compared with the circulation spaces of any public building that facilitates movement – from the massive archetypal American hub airport to Calatrava's cathedral-like railway stations or the urban casbah – is subject to many more influences and interventions. It is therefore much more episodic and varied in its language: from road signs and fascia, furniture and vegetation, to scale, composition, colour variation and lighting. Nonetheless, as a space, the street can still be considered from three perspectives: its operational politics, its modes of use and circulation, and what these reveal to us about how it is understood and experienced as a particular urban territory.

Street space in a city, when viewed *en masse*, is a definitive public environment characterised by a bricolage of façades, and a combination of scale and density. Taken individually, the fact that streets are variegated according to levels of access and the role they play also creates specific identities for each; whilst put together in connected groups, they contribute to the overall identity of an area. In a city like Venice, for instance, with few grand public routes which aren't on the water, that identity isn't due to anything like uniformity, as streetscapes demonstrate a huge diversity of forms and scales, and are named by type: the Venetian *salizzada*, for example, is a paved street; a *calle* is a former pathway; the *rio terra* is a former waterway filled in to give greater strength to the buildings; the *rauro* is a little passage; the *sottoportico*, a covered street under an arcade; and the *lista*, a limited access route leading to an ambassadorial residence, lined with white slabs that mark the limits of diplomatic immunity.

All streets are orchestrated into sequences of the everyday and the scenic. As Kevin Lynch points out in his perceptive and provocative book, *What Time is This Place?* (1972), the best cities are famous for their walks, with streets being perceived as routes to connect dramatic sequences of experiences that link places of contrasting episodic quality. For Lynch, the moving view is the primary way in which we now experience our ▶

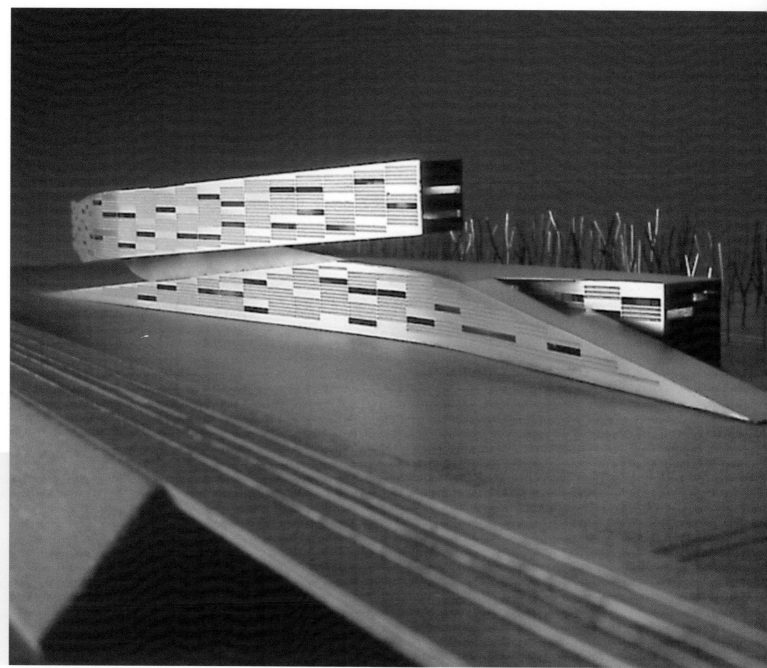

DRIVE-UP
APARTMENT
ALBERTO NICOLAU +
MONTSE DOMINGUEZ

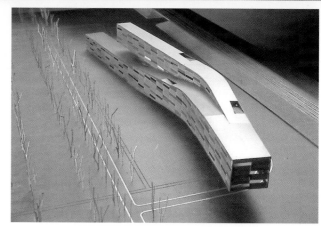

Although it is proposed for a suburban location in Holland, this apartment building by Alberto Nicolau + Montse Dominguez could provide a useful paradigm for housing in a variety of urban settings. In their entry for the fifth Europan competition (for architects up to the age of 40), the architects focused on a site on the outskirts of the city of Almere. An area of flat, reclaimed Dutch land close to the sea, the site occupies a space, according to the architects, between two 'watery planes: the soggy ground and the heavy, damp atmosphere'. In order better to allow residents to appreciate these two zones, the architects, like so many others before them, lift the housing off the ground, placing apartments in huge cantilevered blocks which hang several storeys above the ground at either end of the building.

But the real innovation in Nicolau and Dominguez's project is the acknowledgement that cars have become a vital part of an individual's sense of social identity. Rather than relegating car parking to the street, or to piss-stained underground chambers, Nicolau and Dominguez propose that the apartment block is transformed into a commonly-owned private drive; a ramp to allow cars to be driven up to the level of the owner's apartment. If it sounds like a cross between a multi-storey car park and an apartment block, the reality would be much more civilised. Some cars would be allowed their own private proto-garage space close to the door of the owner's apartment; others would be parked in more traditional car park-style formations, but nonetheless they would be located within a minute's walk of their owner's front door.

Curiously, although the building makes manifest the slope of the ramps which bring the cars inside, the floorplans inside the apartments are horizontal, and in many respects once one reaches the level of the domestic spaces, there appears to be little that distinguishes these apartments from any other. Nonetheless, the project is an impressive first attempt at a building typology which has been little explored in the past thirty years. Although it raises as many questions about residential space and its interface with infrastructure as it answers, Nicolau and Dominguez's apartment block is certain to be joined by further explorations of multi-level, drive-in housing.

environments. Attitudes towards mobility and towards time and change have, as he describes it, substantially increased the potential of what he calls sequence design. He proposes a greater sensing of environmental change, and for time-lapse photography and film to extend our perceptual grasp of city changes through their facility for visual compression. Another idea was the installation on the streets of what Lynch called 'mutoscopes', devices to make invisible processes visible by a mechanism that could 'speed up past and future changes or slow down present vibrations so that we can see them, just as public microscopes and telescopes would extend our perceptual reach'. Predating the development of city streets as sites of global infotainment, and of course the commercialisation of the Internet's virtual superhighways, Lynch's vision extended to using the city as a gigantic teaching device, with automated directories, films and manipulable models, street theatre, and symbols to mark out changes and alternative urban models. Although in making these proposals for a cultural urban outreach programme, he knew full well that the broking of information in the streetscape was an issue of power, maybe Lynch could not have fully anticipated the extent to which commerce would go on to 'site' itself (as it traditionally had done through the street market) in this 'free for all' space.

No single street tells the whole story of the city: all of them are usually necessary for comprehension of where we are, what it is to be in a particular urban territory, as well as for orientation. How far can we say that about the buildings they wrap themselves around? And yet, the streets are more likely to survive even when the individual building is erased; even full-blown demolition of an area will still leave fragile traces. Historically, the streetscape of many cities, Berlin being a particular case in point, has been subject to many different influences, reflecting the reality that cultural development itself is rarely continuous, and so the justification for streets in their own right has gone through many changes of emphasis. As architect Matthias Sauerbruch has commented, 'what typifies Berlin is the motley array of formal languages, street scenes and so on existing in the town. This heterogeneity is not a new phenomenon. From the eighteenth century onwards, the history of the city and its outward manifestations in terms of architecture have been involved in a process of change, layering, contradiction and partial correction. Berlin wears the scars of its history quite openly. There are few cities in Europe that testify so strongly to their history'.

These days, streets are rarely designed collectively as part of grand masterplans. In practical terms, there are few urban sites available for creating such a *tabula rasa*, and ideologically, the notion of an all-encompassing urban strategy has lost its potency. Increasingly, the role of the urban planner in Northern European countries such as the Netherlands, particularly in a city centre like Amsterdam, is becoming one of tuning the inter-relationship between a range of convergent plans and integrating them into an imaginatively-applied organisational concept – one constantly challenged by the many privatising influences to which the public realm

Jean Nouvel's Fondation Cartier in Paris, embraces the street through the delicate transparency of its glass facade.

is subject. Given these conditions, design is as much about the less visible work of keeping public space open through asserting specific relationships between elements, as it is about intervening through form or adhering to tradition. Redefining the urban fabric through formal representations of its past rigidifies the streetscape. As Hans Ebberink, town planner for Amsterdam, explained recently, 'in achieving coherence ... a great deal has been paid to context. This has virtually nothing to do with pursuing local traditions; rather, it is a matter of responding to given conditions with modern means'. Maintaining vistas over historic canals is one such concept; in London, reinforcing the city's relationship with the river by opening up Thameside waterside walks as an extended pedestrian route, might be another way of giving precedence to the streetscape that sits between buildings and the faster transit zones of road or water. Architects embrace the streetscape in various ways, but many do so by the sheer presence of their building alone: think of the sheer, transparent façade of Jean Nouvel's Fondation Cartier in Paris. Similarly, Sauerbruch's practice tries to create buildings that lend themselves to the street, through their amenities, shops, street corner cafés, giving life to public spaces; as he describes it, building an 'urban aura'.

Jane Jacobs richly evoked the street as a site of modernism through the study of its ecology and phenomenology in her book, *The Death and Life of Great American Cities* (1961). Her work describes an urban montage of experiences and rituals: the interaction of friends, acquaintances and strangers, through tracking the 24-hour duration of activity in the street; a lived cycle of real intersecting lives, rather than an aspirational lifestyle. In its various manifestations, the mixed-use street is the place where the Romantic life force, handed down from the era of Haussmann and Baudelaire, is crystallised. It was in the street that Jacobs detected an order, existing in a state of perpetual motion and change, that relied on some preservation of the city of the Haussmann age for the realisation of modern values. Her depictions of the street, and the neighbourhood life of families within the American street block, are microcosms too of global diversity. Marshall Berman, author of *All That is Solid Melts into Air* (1982) (a brilliant account of the experience of modernity), agrees with Jacobs that throughout the Haussmann age and well into the twentieth century, the street was a pre-eminent source of life, 'From the small town 'Main Street' to the metropolitan 'Great White Way' and 'Dream Street', the street was experienced as the medium in which the totality of modern material and spiritual forces could meet, clash, interfuse and work out their intimate meanings and fates' – but one that was being overtaken by another urban agenda which denounced its value.

Berman explains how reconstruction and redevelopment after the Second World War led to a new set of priorities for highway infrastructure, industrial parks, shopping centres and above all for the dormitory suburbs that created wider, less contained networks of urban existence. Streets in the inner cities were either abandoned or actively destroyed. The urban street,

earlier a symbol of promise and progressive modernity, came to denote 'dingy, disorderly, sluggish, stagnant, worn-out, obsolete'. *The Naked City*, the 1948 drama-documentary about detectives at work in New York, vividly conveyed the impression of a city on the point of disappearance as a place directly experienced by pedestrians; abandoned for the suburbs, its localities are dispossessed by urban renewal and dominated by the car. This shift of emphasis to the value of attenuated, decentralised modes of existence has not extinguished the power of the street as a medium of social awareness and movement. Urban planning policies contributed to the coming of a new 'complex order', but so did overall economic changes: today's urban streets are dominated by the rhythms of global capitalism. This complex order is also a physical/virtual hybrid which transformed our sense of time and place. In the eyes of an atomised, mass-mediated public raised on intimate visions of the world offered by television, the street and the direct experiences it offers do not have the intense focus they did in the past. But it does still have a role in the flow of communication, although its role is no longer purely physical as the street now has a new, virtual membrane: the telecommunications that connect every outdoor space with every outdoor space, through all time zones. The street is also a site of speculation in the debate about 24-hour trading, making nocturnal culture an official activity which extends its visible urban life.

Now is the era of post-suburbanism, and in the architectural world the importance of the urban conurbation with its public streets as a flexible fabric in which to shape cultural identity is receiving huge attention. Accordingly, the city street needs to have its episodic, experiential qualities registered artistically, as much in the more gloomy northern hemisphere as it does at say the Rio Carnival. That wish is one to which photographers as well as writers interested in the city are increasingly bringing the subjective languages of the visual arts and the traditionally objective eye of architectural photography, evolved through the developing possibilities of new technologies; imagery of the street takes form as seductive advertising support for new developments. The publication of Jacobs' book coincided with a surge of interest by New York artists in the spaces and objects of everyday life, collecting and transforming junk from the streets, experimenting with three-dimensional environments combining painting, architecture and sculpture, and staging 'happenings': events that spilled human energy beyond their studios and galleries. Artists such as Jim Dine, Red Grooms and Allen Kaprow, but also dancers like Merce Cunningham and Twyla Tharp in the 1960s and 1970s aimed to incorporate the street's qualities of randomness and spontaneity. Artist Claes Oldenburg's aim, as he wrote in 1961, was for a 'political-erotical-mystical art' to spontaneously embroil itself with every day life, and 'come out on top'. This impulse to mirror the city's positive qualities and capture fluid urban experience was reflected by numerous poets and musicians paying homage to the American city street's dramatic and symbolic place in their imaginative landscapes. Jean-Luc Godard's films made the city the central character

in the plot, evocatively conveying the changing light and provoking rhythms of modern Paris.

In *All That is Solid Melts into Air*, Berman describes how this love affair with the urban street foreshadowed the radical politics of the 1960s' use of urban spaces for public dialogue. Describing the development of areas like the Bronx in the 1960s, he conveys how it was 'possessed by the great modern dream of mobility', and 'the easy confidence of our official culture, the civic faith that America could overcome its inner contradictions by driving away from them' – towards an exorable 'expressway world' that constituted the American dream. Berman goes on to explain that it was only in the 1970s when economic growth and expansion stalled (when it became unaffordable to destroy the past) that themes like creative recycling crop up in dilapidated neighbourhoods. In New York, the departure of industrial tenants from the SoHo district led to the use by artists of loft spaces. Eventually, identity was again shown as contingent, and the old industrial streetscape became the territory of a new kind of real-estate speculation, driving many from their nests during the development of what became new urban community.

Architects who have embraced the street are those who have been concerned with patterns of association, as well as vernacular sources of imagery. The Smithsons, for instance, whose interest in the life of the street stemmed from a childhood spent in Glasgow, proposed to replace the four functions of urban life as defined by CIAM (the Congrès Internationaux d'Architecture Moderne) – living, working, recreating and circulating – with four levels or worlds of patterns of association: the house, the street, the district and the city. For them, the development of a new city form needed to recognise the centrality of human association. The Smithsons' 1952 proposal for Golden Lane, a bombed-out area of inner London, proposed a street-deck system not unlike the lines of the main sewers. Its composition was based on the living patterns of inhabitants, including and valuing the shape of 'life in action' rather than on 'the netting of an imposed geometric pattern'. In their investigation of the vernacular, art is part of and not separate from, everyday life; they argued that 'our sense of any single activity can only be made rational by our sense of the whole'.

The paradox is that although it is the city's most quotidian place, in all its contingent formal identity, the street still offers some kind of point of reference. It is the urban territory where no system as such is experienced, but where one finds a sense of the everyday as 'a denominator common to existing systems including judicial, contractual, pedagogical, fiscal and police systems', as Lefebvre described it in 'Quotidien et Quotidienneté (an essay published in 1972). Can a focus on the street transcend the banal? Lefebvre's answer about the everyday applies to any study of the street, which I echo: 'Why should the study of the banal itself be banal? Are not the surreal, the extraordinary, the surprising, even the magical, also part of the real? Why wouldn't the concept of everydayness reveal the extraordinary in the ordinary?'. Indeed – why can't street level be a revealing territory?

REALITY, I FIND ENOUGH REGULAR UNASHAMED JOY IN HUMAN LIFE (DETAILS THAT CANNOT POSSIBLY BE ITEMISED), TO REGARD THE STREET AS MY FRIEND, A PLACE FOR WHICH I DON'T NEED HEADPHONE ACCOMPANIMENT.

RUNNING TRACK
RESIDENCE
DLM ARCHITECTS

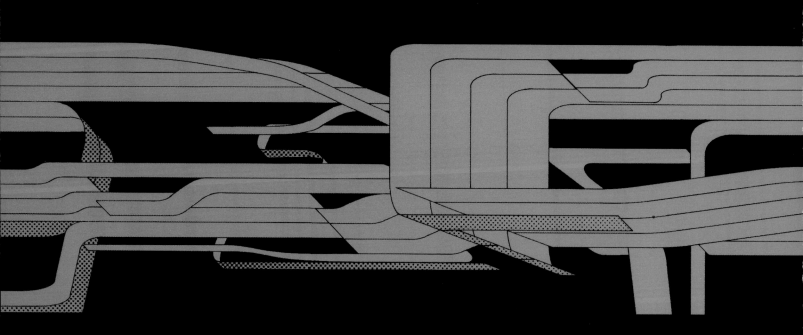

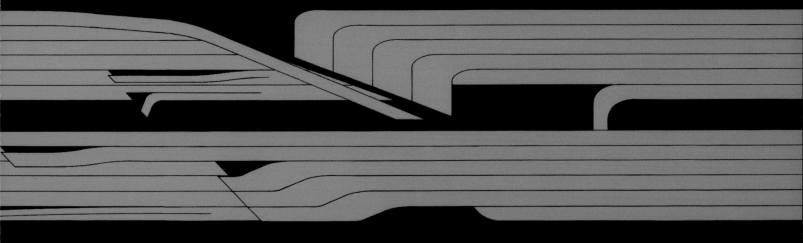

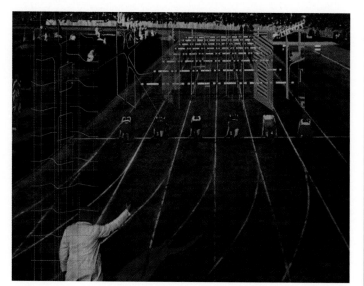

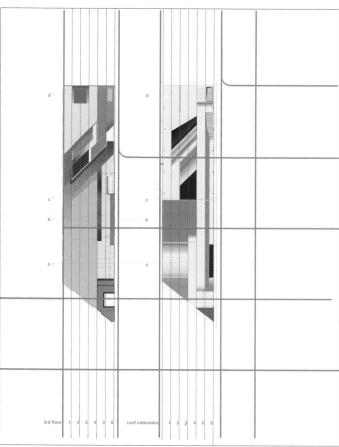

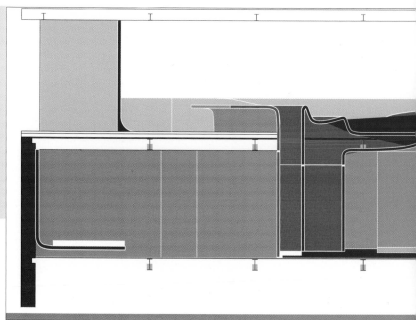

Above right: the plans for
each level of the Running
Track Residence (upper floor
to the left, lower floor to the
right) show clearly how the
apartment is divided into
programmatic strips.
Main picture: the strips are
peeled away to create a
breakfast bar, a room, and even
a desk on the upper level.

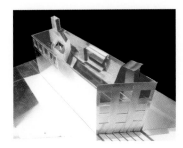

Three architects who recently set up their own practice have developed a project in London which explores ideas about different levels, and folds them into a successful apartment design. Formed in 1999, DLM Architects is made up three partners: Oliver Domeisen, Jee-Eun Lee and Michèle Mambourg. Domeisen, who worked as part of the Foreign Office team that won the Yokohama Ferry Terminal competition in 1995, joined Zaha Hadid's office in 1997, where he met Lee. Together, they project managed the design of a stage set for the Pet Shop Boys, and the exhibition *Addressing the Century* at the Hayward Gallery in London.

While many of Hadid's projects investigated the formal possibilities of stratification, it was the design for the LA Eyeworks retail outlet, in which Domeisen and Lee played a significant role, which saw the office take layering to a logical conclusion, constructing the entire retail space from a series of horizontal strata, and then cutting them away to reveal the retail space within.

For DLM's apartment project, planned for completion in 2001, the architects take this striated plan and turn it on its edge. They divide the long apartment space into a series of strips, each of which is initially allocated a functional programme such as living area, utilities, or circulation. This running-track plan is then partially peeled away (DLM describe it as 'architecture as striptease'), so that the flooring strips are lifted into the air to create walls, tables, and ultimately a series of volumes linked by a ramp. The effect of peeling away is created by laying strips of fibre-reinforced concrete just 15mm thick on the existing floor, and then moulding each strip into the required shape. The concrete will be covered (probably with a coloured resin) to seal in the fibres and give the floor a forgiving feel underfoot. The utilities strip, for example, lifts as it passes through the kitchen area, to become a breakfast bar.

At the opposite edge of the apartment from the utilities space, a strip designated for circulation lifts off the ground to create a ramp which rises up to the apartment's upper level. Here, a new conservatory will be constructed. As the conservatory gives out onto the roof terrace, its floor dips 15cm to create a shallow reflective pool immediately outside the windows, and then rises again beyond the pool to create the outdoor terrace area. Deterministic though this layout may seem, DLM have created some ingenious spatial solutions by deploying this series of programmatic striations – and as a practice they promise to become a serious architectural force.

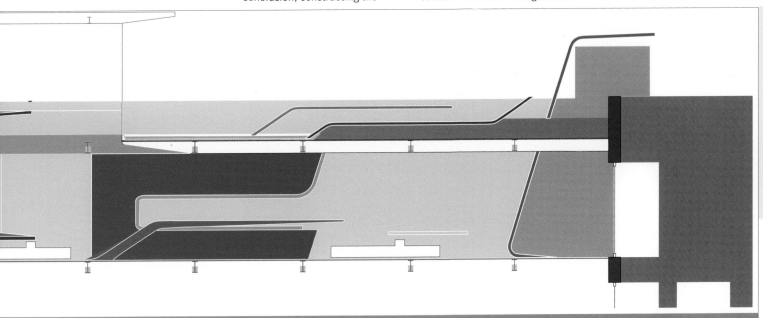

Approached from Shoreditch High Street, the NatWest Tower – Tower 42 to use its correct and more martial designation – rises like a splintered shaft, its two secondary components clinging to the central column for support. It doesn't really have any colour, but even from here its girders, rafts and joints are clearly visible, pressing flatly against a frontage of infinitely reflective, sheeted glass. It is six o'clock on a Monday morning and the bruise-blue, post-dawn light has rendered this part of London tantalisingly immobile.

Outside the DeutscheBank building on Broadgate, a solitary sanitation officer grapples with the mechanics of a water cannon, preparing without enthusiasm to hose away the detritus of an uneventful Sunday night. Three kids in utilitarian clothing drift up Primrose Street; Spanish perhaps, or Portuguese. They're lost but unconcerned, probably recently turfed out of a club in Hoxton.

One of them hop-skotches the cracks in the pavement talking loudly, still battling against an imagined beat. Each of us – me, the kids, the cleaner – has temporary but complete possession of our patch of street and we move, wander really, without constraint. These are the last moments of the night, the dregs of the weekend. The day's third or fourth overland train pulls into Liverpool Street, its rolling stock sighing tiredly. A few moments later, a dribble of commuters emerges from the station and instinctively the three kids regroup into a tighter formation. We're all about to lose our place.

Page 62 of the *London A–Z*, grid references 6D to 6E – the City – is a stunningly dense piece of cartography. You need to screw up your eyes, hold the book up to the light, cross-reference it with the more generously laid-out version on page 142; in its graphic intensity, the bottom-right hand

corner of page 62 might convey nervousness, uncertainty and escalating paranoia: necessary qualities for survival amongst those who work in the strange old-new, productless environment of London's international financial district. But the streets of the City aren't indecipherable merely on paper. They really are hard to read, and difficult to navigate. Narrow, hemmed in and overshadowed, walking their pavements can feel like an act of intrusion; issues of space, access and ownership are all clouded by the self-contained nature of the corporations that flank them. We use the streets to get here. We use the streets to leave. But increasingly reduced to the status of functional thoroughfare or chain-store vestibule, it is no longer clear what other purpose they serve.

In most parts of most towns it's not hard to guess from the street what's going on inside the buildings, but Tower 42 is

a remarkably coy construction, and not merely in the lack of information available to the curious passer-by. Set back from Old Broad Street, it rests on massive concrete cantilevers, its base actually fifty feet up in the air. Standing on the pavement gazing up at the distant apex is enough to induce a sort of sympathetic vertigo, but the narrowness of Old Broad Street – the City is full of such erroneously-named routes – means that from the other side of the road, Tower 42, clearly visible in Acton to the west, or Leyton to the east, is here invisible. You could walk by and never know it was there.

Set into the squat bunker of the Tower's base is the diffidently-named Café Zero. Chrome-fitted and functionally modern, it's open to the public but the atmosphere within is, if not formal then certainly restrained, and clearly subject to the full weight of the forty two storeys pressing down

WALKING THE GRID
JONATHAN FORTGANG

from above. This far, it seems to say, but no further. The distinction between public and private space in the City is, for the most part, clearly delineated, but can have unexpected implications for individual status and identity. One bicycle courier maintains that, dressed in the fluorescent top and Lycra shorts of his profession, he is assured entry into any City firm despite the fact he sports a full range of revolutionary accessories: dreadlocks, tattoos, facial piercing. Once, on a day off, he tried to pay an unannounced visit to his girlfriend who was temping for a major financial organisation. He took five steps across the marble floored vestibule before being wheeled round and ejected by a jittery security officer. Next day, back in Lycra, he was able to wander up to the fifth floor without comment.

At waist-height on a low vault to the left of the Tower 42's entrance, is a Blue Plaque dedicated to Sir Thomas Gresham, founder of The Royal Exchange and identifier of Gresham's law, the financial principle that states bad money drives out good. The Plaque ('In a house on this site lived…') is a beacon for smokers. Damp strands of tobacco spread across the paving like concrete-dwelling worms, the smokers' refusal to give up their patch a distant echo perhaps, of territorial urination. Whether by accident or artful self-reference, the ashtrays located at a dignified distance from the entrance to many City firms bear an uncanny resemblance to the pyramidal tip of Canary Wharf. Similarly, within the bulbs of the area's globular streetlights there appears to be a tiny replica of the Tower. A model-maker's touch, in a model part of town.

A significant casualty though, in the running battle between public and private space at street level is the rubbish bin. Grudging acceptance that a freely-accessible, enclosed metal box might pose a threat to security is not reflected in our attitude towards public hygiene. Our relationship to the street in this respect is furtive: scrunch up a crisp packet and hold it in your hand until an appropriately concealed receptacle presents itself. Stuff or dump or drop your trash, walk on and don't look back. Everywhere, between adjacent telephone boxes, beneath bus shelter seats, behind those metal cupboards in front of which crouch headphone-wearing engineers, in the open ends of scaffolding rods, discreet piles of rubbish blossom like colourful fungus.

At the junction of Old Broad Street and Threadneedle Street is the Stock Exchange. Here, the buildings retreat a little and the sky reappears. It's half-past nine and difficult to resist the tidal pull of pedestrians heading towards Bank, but off to the left at the far end of Old Broad Street is an ▶

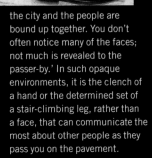

Affairs, Finnish photographer Tuuli Koivisto's documentary study of the hurrying bodies that belong to people flowing round the Bank area of the City of London, relates to the way in which individuals in this most formal of city spaces plot isolated courses through the urban landscape. Koivisto says, 'What interests me is the way the city and the people are bound up together. You don't often notice many of the faces; not much is revealed to the passer-by.' In such opaque environments, it is the clench of a hand or the determined set of a stair-climbing leg, rather than a face, that can communicate the most about other people as they pass you on the pavement.

odd diversion. Adams Court claims to be closed but is in fact open. It's not clear whether this is a private court, or a public thoroughfare. It could be a business or a residence or a hotel or a pub. Attached to the large, wrought-iron gate is a photocopied sign, protected from the elements by a sheet of plastic. It advertises, in faux-Victorian font, a 'Gentleman's Hairdresser'. The price list is headed 'Tariffs'. There are signs like this in shop windows all over the City, all over London, the appeal to antiquity clearly intended as a badge of quality. The gate of a closed and possibly private court seems an odd place to advertise but, since this sign doesn't reoccur, presumably worthwhile.

The court itself is well tended but eerily empty. At one end are some cloisters, and on the ground by a bench is a full glass of red wine. It has the feel of a stage set, a little oasis, but the absence of people induces a strange sort of

anxiety. Partly it's the fear that security guards will appear and demand I explain my presence. And partly it's a sensation akin to those arriving-at-work-with-no-clothes-on dreams: if no one else is here, then why am I? Post Office Court off nearby Lombard Street is another enclosed, deserted passage, but one with all the charm and atmosphere of a subway at 2am. Its walls, featureless slabs of concrete, are thrown into harsh relief by the overhead strip lighting, which buzzes angrily. The floor is pockmarked with urine and vomit stains. This is another side of life at street level: ugly, threatening, anonymous – an arena in which we feel we can act on our basest impulses with impunity. Who cares? No-one lives here. No-one's looking.

Except of course they are. On the streets someone is always looking out for us. On Finch Lane, a CCTV camera swivels infinitesimally as I pass. Usually accompanying these cameras is a sign: '!CCTV

in Constant Operation,' that exclamation-mark prefix suggesting a peculiarly dangerous kind of fun. Most of our time on the street seems to be mediated by glass in one form or another. Visible in the reflective front of the Amro building on Bishopsgate are dim figures with furrowed brows. They scurry onwards then disappear for a while, re-emerging in the shockproof fronts of the shops around Liverpool Street where they rearrange their hair or smooth an unruly eyebrow.

Lunchtime, drifting around the Prets and the Starbucks and the Coffee Republics that line the City's commercial streets. On Wormwood Street fetid air gusts out of waist-height grills; then back down Old Broad Street. At the far end, outside the Stock Exchange, a line of flags flutters triumphantly. Flags are everywhere in the City, their emblems portentous but indecipherable. The only exception is the area around

the Royal Exchange, where signage is approached with almost obsessive discretion. A polished brass plaque with letters no more than an inch high bears a series of quiet inscriptions: 'Global Investment Advisors'; 'Asset Management'; 'Personnel'. They sound like shadowy government agencies. Only Gordon Yates is proud, brave and possibly vulgar enough to declare, 'A Passion for Recruitment.'

Shops too, are reluctant to boast. A little sign in a little window near Bank announces 'Fine shoes.' Shirts are also 'Fine.' So are suits, and cigars, and cheese. Only a shop selling mobile phones is prepared to buck the trend. There the deals are 'Great.' The hurrying, hungry workers are young, or at least young-looking but frequently pensive. Lunchtime, when the offices churn their workers out onto the streets also reveals some of the City's absentees: no children, no pensioners, no beggars, no

Artist Effie Paleologou's photographic work concentrates on capturing images of the city at night, those moments when even the most innocuous elements of the urban environment can be fleetingly transformed into fragments of pavement theatre by a trick of the light – or of the imagination.

animals, no-one asking for a light or a cigarette or the time. Communication occurs within small groups, rarely larger than four, or hurriedly over the phone. So ubiquitous in fact is the mobile phone that at the bottom of Walbrook they've erected a statue in its honour. 'Liffe Trader' stands on the pavement, hips cockily jaunted, top-button undone. Placed there in 1997, he's already embarrassingly dated – his phone is the same size as his feet.

Approached from Lovat Lane (not far from Pudding Lane where the Great Fire of London started in 1666), The Monument looks tiny, dwarfed by Tower 42, the belligerent-looking Lloyds Building, the blue glasshouse of HSBC and all the other heroic constructions that make up the City's spiked skyline. A little flowerbed sits at the bottom of Lovat Lane, a single tree flanked by an eruption of colourful but stunted shrubbery. When the Great Fire started, the Lord Mayor,

Sir Thomas Budworth came to the scene and declared that 'a woman might piss it out'. The same might be said of this ill-looking tree, the chief function of its surrounding earth being to receive the lager-enhanced urine of late-night drinkers with a long walk to the tube.

But The Monument is still impressive, with Wren's glinting golden flame drawing the eye involuntarily upwards to the top. At its entrance is a sign confidently declaring that climbing it will offer the best view of London. Of course it's not. It's just a great view of London, but the City Council's unquenchable pride in The Monument is evident in the retention of that emphatic definite article. It is 202-feet high, a vertical extent which exactly matches the distance from its base to the site where the Great Fire started. One American guidebook firmly reminds its readers that there is '...no elevator'. But then the same

book, published only six years ago, also provides an English-into-American dictionary in which the American word umbrella becomes the English word 'bumbershoot'. The London this guide describes is surreally, archaically peculiar – worth a visit, one imagines.

Climbing the 311 steps up to the viewing platform though, is rather lift-like. Such windows as there are are small and cloudy, so that apart from breathlessness there's little sense of a change in altitude. Out on the caged platform at the top, it's a little crowded, but quiet. The Monument may be less than a third of the size of Tower 42, but the view provides a brief sense of perspective to which the most eloquent response seems to be silence, although graffiti on the skin of the stone speaks mostly of self-aggrandizement: 'Marco was 'ere'; 'Peachy is the best'; 'I am the best'; 'We rule'.

The weather has turned and the sky is a dismal grey, heavy

with the city's waste. Around us are the landmarks that define London to tourists but which most of us who live here never get round to visiting: HMS Belfast, St Paul's, Battersea Power Station. A cloud of viscous smoke with no visible source drifts across the river, briefly obscuring the view back to Tower 42. This is a rare moment in which the City isn't defined by its purpose; from up here it's possible to discern patterns and regularities in the arrangement of streets below. On the other side of the platform, some French kids take pictures of each other. They huddle together around the central plinth, embracing one another and laughing. They are gloriously oblivious to the view, knotted together so that no one can pass. They were there when I arrived and there when I left, gazing up and across the city – but not down.

Smokers, a set of photographs taken by artist Louise Dignand charts the shifty territorialism of office workers forced to indulge their habit in the democratic but banal spaces tucked back off the city's pavements

Zaha Hadid's most important built project to date, a new centre for the exhibition of science, will be situated in a strategically important location at the heart of Wolfsburg. Part exhibition space, part filter between the residential city and its huge adjoining car factory, Hadid's building (due for completion in 2001) derives its formal and functional power from the astute division of each of its levels into public or private space – and then by driving a glass access tunnel right through the building which is accessible to the public 24 hours a day.

The town of Wolfsburg provides an important background to the logic of Hadid's building. In 1938, Hitler needed an 'exemplary German workers' town' to manufacture his 'strength through joy' car, the VW Beetle. Urban planning was by Albert Speer – following the principles of the Garden City movement – and the key to the plan was the separation of the town's industrial area from its domestic and leisure zones. This was made more overt by accentuating the town's existing topography, placing industry to the north of the Mittelland canal, and the residential area to the south.

To the north of the canal, construction commenced on the largest car factory in the world. South of the river, several significant buildings were completed after the war, including three cultural centres by Alvar Aalto (1962–8): the theatre by Hans Scharoun (1973), and the Art Museum by Schleger and Partner, completed in 1994. For fifty years, Speer's split between culture and industry remained as powerful as ever.

Today, things are different. Fundamental changes in the automotive industry have seen companies such as VW shift from a focus on manufacturing, to a focus on service. These changes have heralded a new approach in Wolfsburg: a zone dedicated to the celebration of automotive culture

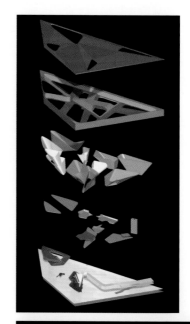

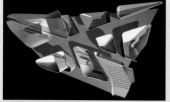

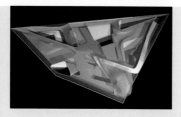

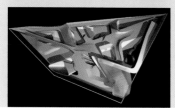

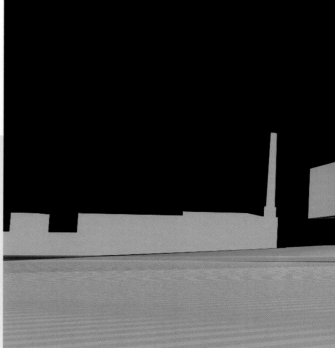

WOLFSBURG SCIENCE CENTRE
ZAHA HADID

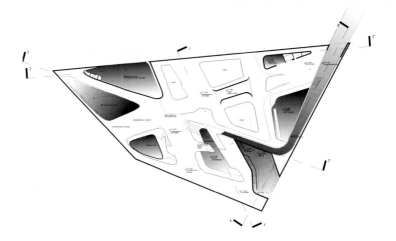

within the industrial northern part of the city. For the first time, the need to link the distinct parts of the city has become more than simply a matter of getting workers to and from the factory each day. Zaha Hadid's design for the Science Centre, located as it is on the southern bank of the canal, will act as a key filtering mechanism between the two zones, and its primary conceit is to encourage flow – through the heart of the building – by the sensitive programming of its different levels.

Hadid's design uses the traditional modernist device of raising a building off ground level on pilotis. However, these are no Corbusian stilts, but hollow conical supports which take the weight of the building above and allow for vast spans over the open spaces at ground level. At the same time, they act as circulatory elements, housing escalators and stairs to give access to the exhibition spaces above. Equally importantly, the placement of these conical feet has been carefully selected so as to allow clear sightlines through the building. Important axes such as that of the main pedestrianised Porsche Strasse, or from the nearby railway station through to the town centre, are continued between the cones to generate public space beneath the building. And with the first level an impressive seven metres above ground, this public space will be no dark undercroft. Hadid has provided for a restaurant and other retail spaces to be housed inside the cones, and special attention is being paid to lighting the space using both natural and artificial light sources.

Enter the building through one of its cones, and you will be carried upward to first floor level, with immediate views out over the south of the city. The main exhibition space of the building is located at this level, but cutting through it is an inclined glass tunnel/ramp which is completely inaccessible from inside the building. It is a tunnel which acts as a new exit ramp from the town's only footbridge over the canal. By drawing visitors through the building, Hadid makes it impossible for anyone travelling between the factory and the town to miss the cultural display of scientific knowledge in the building's exhibition space. The inaccessibility of the tunnel from within the exhibition spaces, however, means that its function as a generator of human flow is also a powerfully symbolic one: visitors to the scientific exhibitions will see human beings moving relentlessly through the biggest glass display case of all, and human flow will become the building's proudest exhibit.

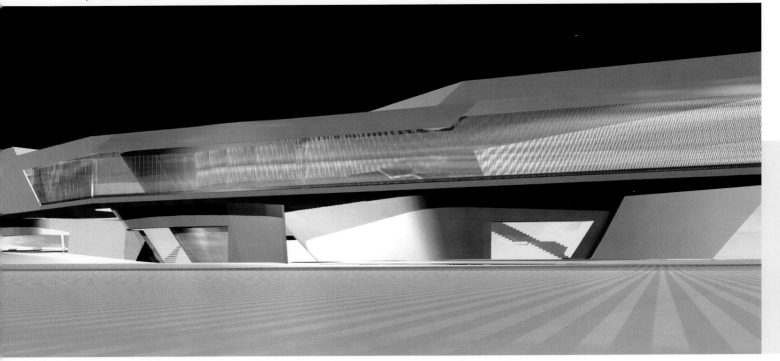

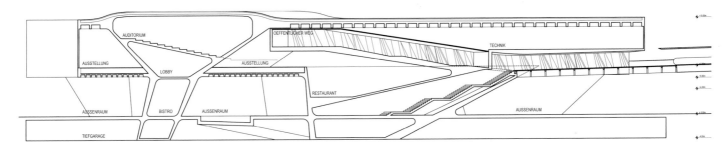

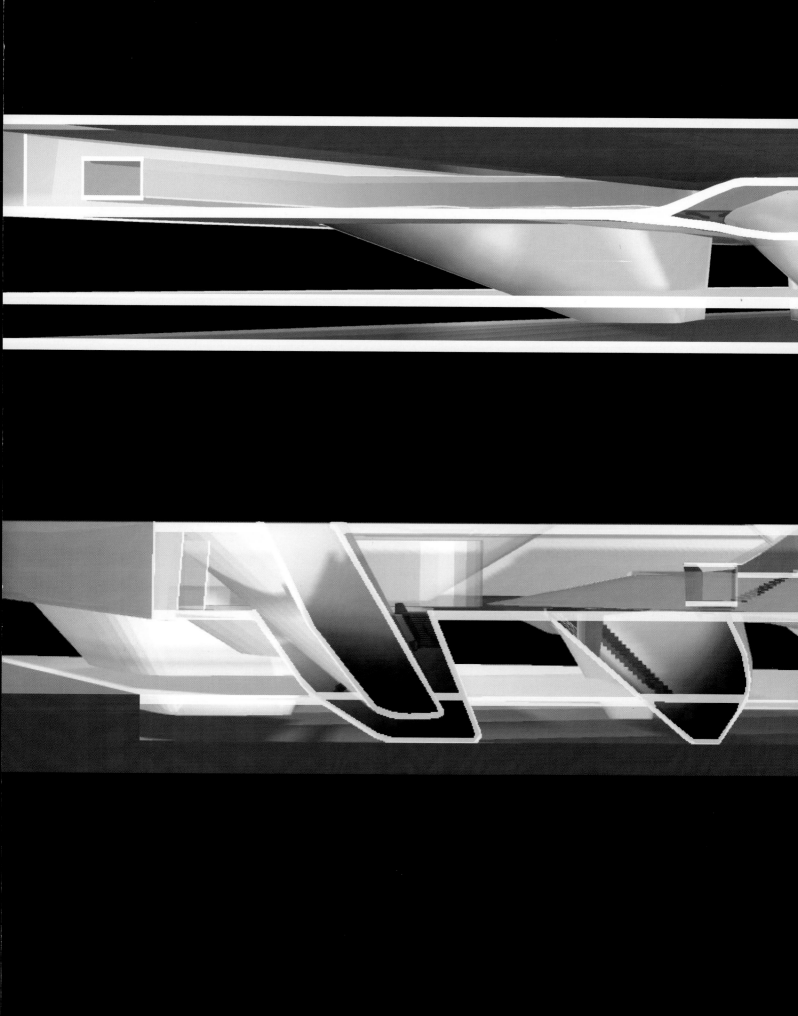

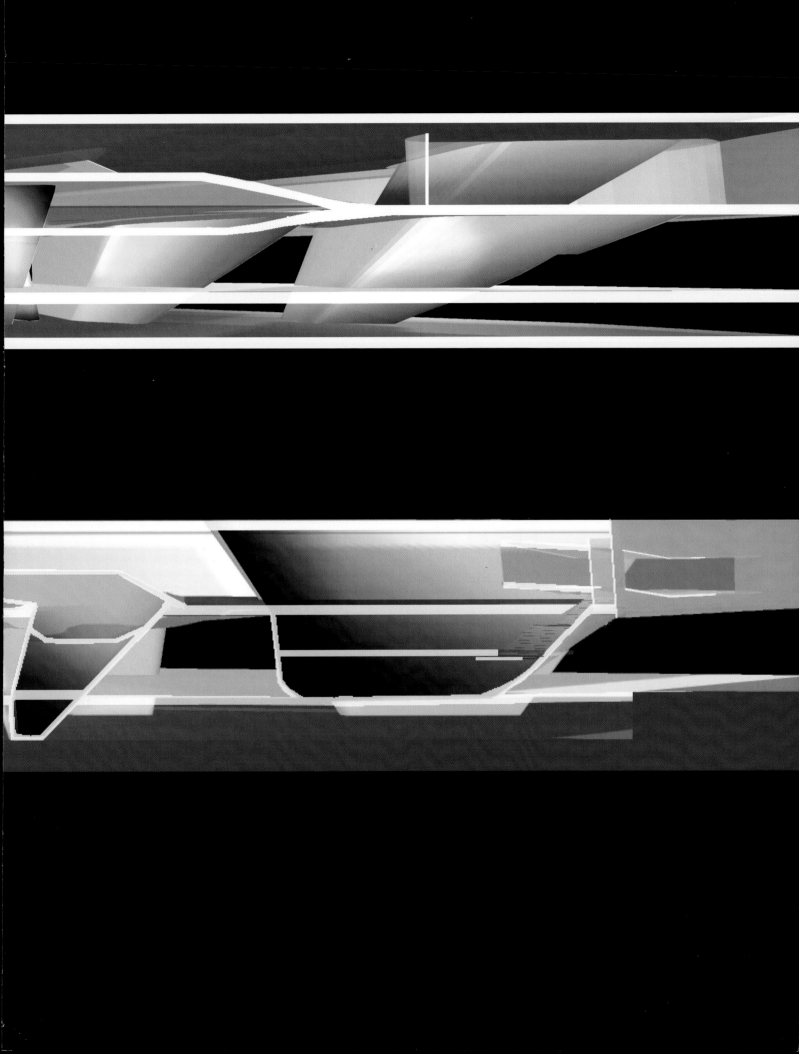

WALKING IS READING
EYAL WEIZMAN, MANUEL HERZ

Among the applications submitted to the London Borough of Barnet Planning Department in 1991 was a proposal to erect approximately thirty gates composed of a pair of metal poles with fishing line stretched between. Placed above road junctions and between walls and fences, these would close the gaps in a continuous boundary within the borough. The application had been submitted by the United Synagogue on behalf of the orthodox Jewish community of Barnet. It proposed that on the Jewish Sabbath, within the marked boundary – a space called the 'eruv' (the Hebrew term for mixing) – public and private territories would be blended to create a private space the size of a town.

In 1988, Rabbi Allen Kimche of London's Ner Yisroel Community had invited Rabbi Eider, an American authority on 'eruvim', to help him devise a plan for an eruv adapted to the specific conditions of the city's northern

anti- and pro-eruv groups were formed, lawyers were hired, petitions gathered, and letters written. It became clear that the Barnet eruv was to have to deal with more than just tuning a religious concept to suit the material condition of the city.

The theological basis of the eruv is centred on a unique relationship between territory and space, informed by the two poles of existence which define the geographical matrix of Jewish history: kingdom and desert. Mediating between the two, the eruv gives them a shared urban form. For a nomadic people in search of a promised land, the desert – the ultimate state of placelessness – becomes a unifying condition which leads to the pursuit of a place and stability. The nomad's space (his place) is not tied to a specific location. Thus the notion of place had to be divorced from a fixed geographical definition. The eruv is a means of creating such an abstract notion of space: a

Temple, a door measuring ten cubits seperated the mundane from the holy, the public area from the private. The Devir was the most private space, where only the high priest was allowed to enter, once a year. A 'public' domain is defined as an area like a thoroughfare that is frequented daily by 600,000 people (referring to the number of Israelites encamped in the desert). Thus, on the Sabbath, the eruv transforms the city into a representation of the Temple, turning it from a public into a private domain. If the eruv area is understood as the Temple of Jerusalem, the outer area is the desert, and movement into the eruv is an act of wandering that culminates in the appropriation of a place.

The eruv uses a chain of signifiers to turn the city into private space. The ultimate private space is the Devir, thus it is necessary to build the Temple over the city. Because of the

These images were recorded during the course of a single Sabbath, on a round-the-clock walk Eyal Weizman took along the 11.5 miles of the Barnet eruv's perimeter in September 1999.

suburbs. They walked and studied the streets of Barnet, and sketched out a boundary for an eruv covering an area of six-and-a-half square miles encompassing Hendon, Golders Green and Hampstead Garden Suburb. The Barnet Council Planning Department had no idea of how to deal with the rabbis' proposal. The eruv did not fall into any of the usual categories of construction: no land had to be acquired, and as the boundary was of a purely symbolic nature, no access to infrastructure was needed. Nevertheless, the Council decided that planning permission was required. When the eruv proposal was published, it provoked an unprecedented public reaction:

dynamic, private and portable zone which can be deployed in cities all over the world, as a means of re-establishing the Temple in a conceptual form.

The domains of the eruv are defined in terms of signifiers relating to the city and the desert. These definitions disregard the actual use and ownership of urban spaces, and rely completely on their representational aspects: the shapes, sizes and the elements which constitute their boundaries. A 'private' domain is defined as an area enclosed by partitions no less than ten cubits (approximately 4.5 metres) high or bounded by a trench ten cubits deep and four wide. In the Jewish

technical difficulties of doing so, the notion of a roof is substituted for the Temple. The method used to signify a roof over the city is to make a wall around it. Every walled space has openings in it. In the representation of the roof, doorways are therefore equivalent to walls: a series of doorways represents a continuous solid wall. So, symbolically, the eruv changes the nature of urban space. As the definition of space transforms and mutates, so too do the laws bound to it. Jewish law forbids a whole range of work on the Sabbath: formal employment as well as travel, the spending of money, and the carrying of objects outside the home. Movement in public spaces on this day is severly restricted, but if an urban space is designated as private, movement and carrying become permissible. Public space is therefore no longer the space of exchange and activity but a restrictive space of limitation; whereas private space, expanded to include the public domain, becomes the space of liberation and interaction. In the case of the eruv it does not, however, entail ownership. In terms of Jewish law, the eruv space is symbolically private, but in terms of civil law it remains public – its symbolic system is an open discourse.

Guidelines recommend that the eruv should be an integral part of the city, and invisible to the untrained eye. For the Barnet eruv, Rabbi Kimche and Rabbi Eider tried to establish criteria for sensitively incorporating a boundary into the streets. They sought out existing elements of the urban fabric that could be used to signify the periphery, studying boundaries haphazardly created

concept, and the posts and wire that were to be erected – the only part of the scheme that actually required permission. The proposal was examined by the Public Works Committee (PWC), and forwarded to the Town Planning Committee with a recommendation for approval. But in response to the public furore, the Committee refused the application, on the grounds that it would constitute 'a disturbance to visual amenity'. On 27 October, an appeal against non-determination was submitted to the Secretary of State for the Environment. There followed a public hearing allowing all sides a chance to put forward their arguments. Finally, more than six years after members of Ner Yisroel had mapped out the eruv's boundaries, the Department of the Environment announced that the inspector had recommended approval of the project. On 20 September 1994, the recommendation was upheld by the Secretary of State for the

People can, and do, object to being bearers of meanings that mean nothing to them. But behind this is the fact that people often confuse property rights with rights to signification, for instance when someone rejects the idea of the facade of his house becoming part of the eruv 'wall' – for him, his facade belongs to him alone; the eruv threatens to contaminate the space of private property with the public signs of an alien practice.

In fact, of course, one group's use of objects and space as signs does not preclude their use by any other group. In the case of the north-London eruv, different understandings of space and territory, ownership and meaning made it difficult for the public to enter into a pluralism where objects and spaces could be subjected to more than one reading, as in the case where it was proposed that the walls of a church form part of the eruv's perimeter. But it would be wrong to suggest that the eruv

between the public and private domain, the eruv offers the Jewish community social liberation and an increase in the use of and interaction within the public sphere. It proposes interventions in the city which are small-scale, strategic and for the most part non-material, intervening by means of decisions about readings of the city, rather than reconstructing it so that it may be re-read. By providing a model for pluralist uses of the city, the eruv has lessons to teach the Western city in terms of the economy of significations, boundaries, and distinctions between inside and outside, on the one hand, and the scarcity of buildings and land on the other. The conception of the temple appropriates a symbolic urban private space within the homogeneity of the urban desert, which lacks all signification. Such a reading is made possible by the way Jewish law defines the city: it assumes it does not exist in its physical embodiment alone, and

by the raw material of the city. The fencing along the Northern Line railway between East Finchley and Mill Hill marked one, as did that of the M1 motorway, and Hampstead Heath; streets and main roads with continuous terraced housing were chosen to constitute others. For one day of each week these were to represent the walls of the Temple. The chosen perimeter was breached at thirty-one points, where symbolic doorways made of transparent fishing wire were to create the necessary continuous circuit.

The proposal for the North-London eruv that was submitted to Barnet Council on 3 August 1992 made an important distinction between the eruv as a religious

Environment.

Planning law only interrogates structures and their material measurable effect. A discussion about the nature of an eruv never arose during the interrogation. The dialogue was purely concerned with the structure and form of the signifying elements, the eruv's use, shape and effect. Why is the notion of the eruv so problematic for the general public? Partly because of the obvious fact that a minority within the city proposes to determine an aspect of the meaning and use of public space and the objects within it. Unlike other religious practices, which usually take place within private space, the eruv takes rituals and signs into the public sphere.

constitutes a form of symbolic imperialism as, paradoxically, it is only imperialism which insists that an object can mean only one thing, and that a boundary must be observed by everyone. In the polyglot, multicultural city, readings of space and place do not have to be linked to a territory and urban organization; the act of communal interpretation brings to the city's fabric an increase of meaning, rather than a reduction. At the heart of this problem is not the question of imposing upon urban space an obscure religious practice, but rather the willingness of authorities to sanction the city as the site of multiple readings.

By eliminating the difference

that its material elements are always pointing towards something else. Thus the eruv bridges two cities: one that is perceived and tangible, the other, aesthetically ideal – a second metaphorical city is overlaid upon the existing one by the practice of moving through the city. The intervention occurs mainly between the physical elements and their signification, the space and its laws and programme. In temporarily resurrecting the Temple out of the desert of the modern city, the Jewish eruv demonstrates how the material and the metaphoric encounter each other in urban spaces.

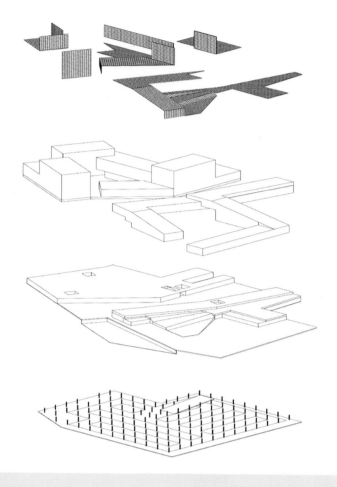

S333 have designed two new city blocks, 'Schots 1 & 2' (meaning 'iceberg' in Dutch) for the town of Groningen, which re-evaluate the urban residential condition. Believing that housing can no longer solely be a problem of mass production of identical stacked apartment units, 'Schots 1 & 2' strive to provide choice and quality at every level for the urban dweller. Writer Harm Tilman in a recent article in *De Architect* suggested that Schots 1 & 2 can be seen as a contemporary example of the 'Megaform', a term first used in 1965 by Fumihiko Maki and Masato Ohtaka. Another writer, Kenneth Frampton, in a 1999 lecture, 'Megaform as Urban Landscape', attempted to give a historical lineage to the term. He concluded that the Megaform is a building of such a scale that it becomes an urban form where one can no longer discriminate between building and landscape. It is a large complex system that extends

horizontally: a form capable of inflecting the existing urban landscape; a form that is not free-standing but which acts as a continuation of the surrounding topography, and finally, a form that orientates itself towards the densification of the urban fabric.

Schots 1 & 2 are conceived as large urban forms sculpted by the existing movement, flows and sight lines working in and around the site. Housing, shopping, recreation, and parking occupy vertically-organised plateaux whilst movement between them is mostly horizontal. This is complemented by a network of roof gardens, and courtyards. Schots 1 & 2 form an alternative to having to choose either the terrace house, the courtyard block or the apartment tower by creating a true mix of all of them. This new hybrid structure is certainly large. Its designers calculate that it offers a wide range of combinations for mixed-use, different materials, and landscapes (the project boasts

SCHOTS
HOUSING PROJECTS
S333

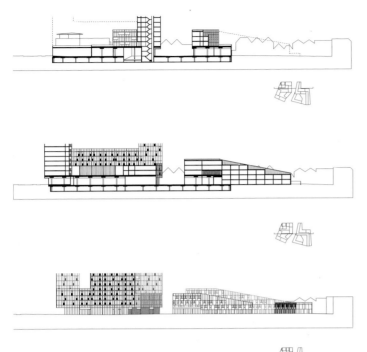

no less than 300 parking spaces, 110 winter gardens, 105 apartments, 44 houses, 14 patios, as well as collective roof gardens, vertical gardens, courtyards, supermarkets, a police station, a playground and a glazed arbour).

Context, nature and the urban ecology have repositioned themselves as grouping and generating forces in the re-evaluation of housing as an ongoing concern for the development of our city landscapes. Rather than landscape being purely considered as something between architecture, S333 interweave it here to create a voluminous silhouette for the city.

Although Schots 1 & 2 are connected by an underground parking lot, and at street level with supermarkets and smaller shops, they evolve quite separately. Schots 1, a robust multi-storey block, is clad entirely in floor-to-ceiling windows where a pattern is created by using different types of glass with varying levels of transparency, reflection, opacity, and colour. In Schots 2, the housing above is accessed by a sloped ground surface that makes a seamless and landscaped transition from street level to a new ground level above, and is entirely clad in large, clear-stained cedar panels. This manipulation enables Schots 1 & 2 to deliver 45 different dwelling types ranging from live/work apartments to five-storey townhouses.

In effect, the reclaiming of Megaform enables S333 to explore a richer spectrum of experience for the city dweller beyond the lift lobby and the balcony. The multi-layering of activities and landscape offer an alternative to the interiorised and hermetic world of the traditional urban block.

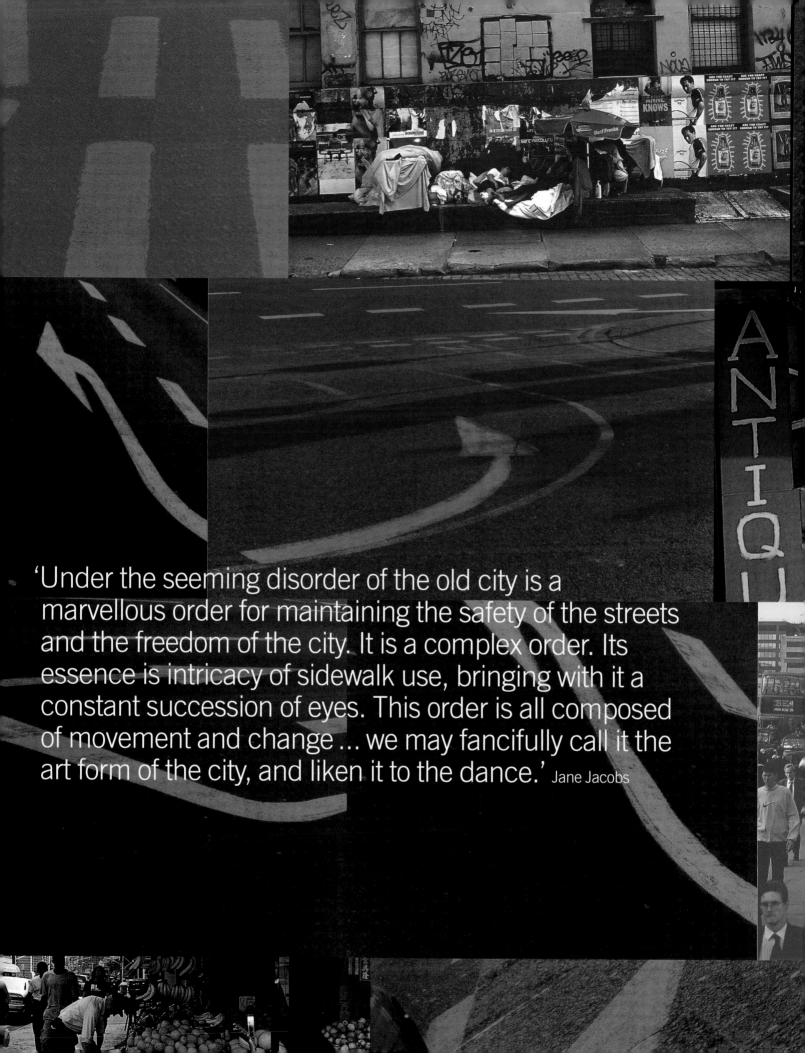

'Under the seeming disorder of the old city is a marvellous order for maintaining the safety of the streets and the freedom of the city. It is a complex order. Its essence is intricacy of sidewalk use, bringing with it a constant succession of eyes. This order is all composed of movement and change ... we may fancifully call it the art form of the city, and liken it to the dance.' Jane Jacobs

Beneath ground

ANGUS CARLYLE

'And so, long live the underground… Eh! But here, too, I'm lying!
Lying because I myself know, like two times two, that it is not at all the
underground that is better, but something different, completely different,
which I thirst for but cannot ever find. Devil take the underground!'[1]

Adopting the view from above does not depend on scaling the heights of
the city's upper levels, but has become a generalised perspective, one which
posits 'verticality' as the key axis of the urban environment. French critic
Henri Lefebvre (widely regarded as responsible for the introduction of
the dimension of space into twentieth-century thought) believes that this
emphasis on verticality tends to produce homogeneity; to the extent that
an edifice is constructed with upward momentum, it abstracts from

the local specificity of the territory on which it is built: 'Verticality, and the independence of volumes with respect to the original land and its peculiarities are, precisely, produced'.[2] Lefebvre and other theorists such as Michel de Certeau[3] argue for replacing a perspective that focuses on elevation with one that engages more readily with ground level and the dynamics of the pedestrian city. Yet the process of levelling the heights of urban prestige needn't stop at the street. An effort can be made to broaden – or more literally, to deepen – our perspective on cities, to force a spatial down-turn which discovers that beneath the pavement there is not only the Situationist's beach ('*Sous les pavés, la plage*'), but the underground. Out of the tunnels, the caverns and the bunkers, will emerge a shadowy architectural figure that has the potential to problematise some of the contemporary conventions of spatial design; 'Ghosts, pockets, traces, necessary clouds: subversion must produce its own chiaroscuro'.[4]

Tunnel visions

'The high gained from such subterranean exploration is so fucking intense there's no need for a chalice in this Wonderland. Unequalled by anything on surface level, the bowels of the city are a sight to behold'.[5]

It is not only the theorists of urban space for whom the underground is something of a lost dimension. For most of a city's inhabitants, it remains a territory defined by abstraction. This fact contributes to the popularity of discovery-style books such as *London under London*, whose authors point out that, 'Every time we turn on the tap, pull the chain, pick up the telephone, there is an underground movement; a gurgle of water, an impulse along a wire … As we bask in the electric sunshine of our city surface, we are quite unaware of the subterranean labyrinth beneath our feet. Very occasionally … we become aware of this troglodyte city … In our everyday lives, our ignorance of the world below extends to profound depths'.[6] The underside of London is made up of a meshwork woven from utilities piping and waste dispatch systems, entwined with the bricked-over channels of the 'lost rivers' (such as the Westbourne and the Fleet), and suspended in a seam made from demolished buildings, domestic and industrial refuse and human remains. Writer Andrew Davies describes London in cross-section as being 'rather like a cake that has risen gently over the centuries … [a] cake [with] many layers'. The nature of some of these buried amenities might be regarded as corroborating the inspirational interdisciplinary thinker, Gaston Bachelard's binary opposition between the 'rationality' of elevated space and 'the dark entity … the one that partakes of subterranean forces … the irrationality of the depths'.[7] However, beneath the pavements lies not only the functional equivalent of the repressed and the unconscious, but also what can perhaps be regarded as analogues of the ego-superego apparatus: the communication networks (including in London, the Post Office's underground rail circuit) and the transport facilities.

Moreover, we should remember that the parameters of use for these tunnel and pipe networks need not be defined only by the civic amenity functions for which they were constructed. For example, sewer systems have provided accommodation for refugees from a variety of troubles. The story

1. Fyodor Dostoevsky, *Notes from Underground*, trans. Richar Pevear and Larissa Volukhorsky, Vintage, London 1993, p.7
2. Henri Lefebvre, *The Production of Space*, Blackwells, Oxford 1991, p.337
3. Michel de Certeau, *The Practice of Everyday Life*, University of California Press, Berkeley and Los Angeles 1987, pp.91–3
4. Roland Barthes, *Le Plaisir du Texte*, Editions du Seuil, Paris 1973, p.53
5. Subterranean London in *Graphotism* Issue 18, 1999, p.24
6. Richard Trench and Ellis Hillman, *London under London*, John Murray, London 1985, p.7
7. Gaston Bachelard, *The Poetics of Space*, The Beacon Press, Boston, Mass. 1994, p.17
8. Jean Baudrillard, 'Kool Killer, or the Insurrection of Signs' in *Symbolic Exchange and Death*, Sage, London 1995, pp.76–85

of Harry Lime's inhabitation of the Vienna sewers in Graham Greene's *The Third Man* was informed by the authenticated accounts of thousands of people who sheltered in tunnels under the city until the middle of the last century. Today, sewer systems continue to represent a last-ditch habitat for the desperate. In Ulan Bator in Mongolia, the manholes that connect to the sewerage and heating system offer relative warmth compared to the surface of a capital city that is the coldest in the world. Recent reports indicate that this has led to a situation where many of Ulan Bator's nearly 3,000 street children live in these subterranean spaces, with up to six inhabiting each manhole. Although offering some shelter and the opportunity to solicit charitable donations from passing pedestrians, the holes' inhabitants are afflicted by a staggering range of diseases and infections.

In spite of the British government's initial hostility to the spontaneous redesignation of tube station complexes as air-raid shelters during the Blitz, it eventually supported the initiative, and other areas of the Underground network were exploited as secure spaces (including a three-mile section of the Central Line, which was turned into a makeshift aircraft component factory). However, the reappropriation of underground transport systems does not always enjoy official sanction, a fact graphically represented in Walter Stern's pop video for The Prodigy's *Firestarter* (1998). In the film, the damaged pastoral evoked by the sleeve illustrations for the group's previous album (which began with a vocal sample announcing 'I've decided to take my work back underground to stop it falling into the wrong hands') is obliterated by the rigorously sustained *mise-en-scène* of the service tunnel. The clip is redolent of the environment of those often derogatorily termed as 'molemen', the people who live in the New York subway system. Estimates of the population size of this community range between 1,000 and 5,000; this after concerted efforts by the Manhattan authorities to restrict access, to render suitable resting places inhospitable (through installing intense overhead lights and sealing alcoves) and to encourage stubborn occupants of this dangerous netherworld to return to the surface and the structure of an outreach programme.

The *Firestarter* video is also suggestive of a more transitory transgression of the city's underground utilities: that mounted by graffiti writers. Jean Baudrillard's prescient essay 'Kool Killer' (first published in 1976), addresses graffiti as 'the end of the repressive space-time of urban transport systems', a 'free and wide-ranging offensive' whose practices 'care little for architecture; they defile it, forget about it and cross the street'.[8] Yet, rather than seeing graffiti as indifferent to architecture, it can perhaps be positioned as something which can inspire an alternative approach to the built environment. In graffiti-space, existing surfaces become vulnerable to optical rescrambling. This can exceed merely recolouration or refiguration and extend to introducing what are apprehended by passing commuters as new textures, new planes or even new depths to the underground canvas. Furthermore, graffiti's navigation of space – in Baudrillard's piece, the space of the submerged rail routes of New York – is as important as its alteration of space. Before their spray cans are triggered, the writers have frequently engaged in an intricate negotiation of the system of tunnelways. This

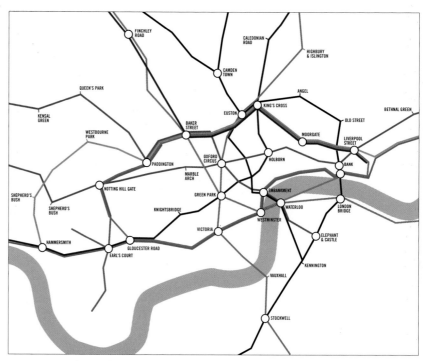

negotiation depends upon such diverse tactics as stealing access door keys; avoiding surveillance cameras, trip-wires, transport police and a possible sentence for criminal damage; manoeuvring around live rails and overhead cables with the very real possibility of injury or even fatality; adjusting to the extremes of silence and deafening noise, bright corridors and pitch-black stairwells; and, fundamentally, developing an intimate knowledge of a labyrinthine system in which 'what were once ignored [become] openings to underground frontiers: manhole covers, push-backed doors, and tunnel entrances all brought a brave new cradle of humanity to our attention'.[9] Thus not only can the geography generated by graffiti transfigure the mundanity of the underground transport network through the graphic stimulation of its sombre surfaces, but potentially, it could activate all of the city's hidden levels as dynamic spaces through the substitution of prosaic, functional value with a new type of usage.

While architectural design's approaches to what might be termed the 'civic' underground are diverse, it is possible to discern a prominent imperative that can be described as the light-bringer aesthetic. Foster and Partners' tube station for Canary Wharf in the Docklands area of London (a structure which occupies the drained West India Dock) powerfully demonstrates this methodology. In this design, signature high-tech elements are deployed to engineer what has been described as 'like a cross between Canterbury cathedral and the set of *Aliens*', as offering 'an almost religious experience'.[10] The interplay of the arcs, angles and vectors of glass and steel operate to attract and then multiply the available light. This mechanism can also be seen in two relatively recent entrance structures to underground complexes designed by I M Pei; one for the extension to the Louvre in Paris, one for the Miho Museum in Kyoto. To a certain extent, these projects can be interpreted as attempts to expel the underground's darkness and ambivalence. While there are clearly justifications for trying to eliminate

9. Mark Sinckler and Ephraim Webber, 'Pushing Back the Doorways' in *Graphotism* Issue 17, 1999, p.31
10. Andrew Smith, 'Tubeway Armies', *The Observer*, 7 November 1999, p.28
11. Bernard Rudofsky, *Architecture Without Architecture: A Short Introduction to Non-Pedigreed Architecture*, Academy Editions, London 1964, p.19

the obscurity of the underground – not least questions of personal safety – it is regrettable that ultimately, the universal application of these principles would erode any distinction between surface and deep locations spaces and banish the shadow as a contributory element to lived space.

Subterranean homesick blues

Although it could be anticipated that only the most industrially sophisticated and financially secure could pursue a subterranean existence, it is actually possible to take a low-tech approach to living below the earth. But as architectural analyst Bernard Rudofsky suggests, low-tech does not necessarily 'imply a low cultural level'. The picture of the caveman dragging his mate by the hair is a cartoonist's cliché, betraying nostalgia for bygone days rather than a portrait of the kind of people who prefer to live underground'.[11] If historically, troglodytism was frequently a response to persecution, geographically, its distribution is widespread: from the enormous residential cave at Shandiar in the Zagros Mountains of Iraq, through the mud domes covering the bazaars of Séojare in Iran, the underground cities of Cappadocia in Central Turkey carved out of the tufa which evolved from volcanic ash, the multi-storied 'troglodyte town' of Pantalica in Sicily, to the subterranean settlements of Andalucia in Spain, the indigenous American tribal structures detailed by William Morgan, and the schools, factories, hotels, and government institutions that lie below the rich fields of Tungkwan in Hunan Province, Southern China. The Chinese example indicates that this kind of lifestyle is still feasible in a modern world; and thousands of people still remain in the Cappadocian caves in Turkey despite the area having been designated a national park, being subject to strict planning controls, and suffering an influx of inquisitive tourists.

From the 1950s onwards, the Egyptian architect Hassan Fathy and, in the late 1970s, Japanese architect Kisho Kurokawa, conducted experiments in developing enclosed dwellings designed with a sensitivity to North-African climatic conditions and the regional vernacular; Fathy in a great number of locations, and Kurokawa at Al-Srir in Libya. Their officially-sanctioned projects can be identified as an extension of archaeological historian Barbara Jones' concept of the 'overground underground' that she applied to surface funerary monuments which nonetheless exhibited characteristics ordinarily attributable to below-ground constructions. That is, Fathy's and Kurokawa's distinct structures offer intimations of a surface architecture which has absorbed something of the interplay of texture and light typically redolent of the underground. Yet these dwellings are officially sanctioned and remain firmly located on the surface of the earth, so as such, perhaps more viable candidates to express the architectural inheritance of the troglodyte tradition are the UK anti-road protestors' tunnel systems, which are designed to prevent the rapid clearance of land marked for redevelopment. Yet these earthworks represent only one dimension of subterranean accommodation, the other dimension – unlike the 'geotectures' of the troglodytes – depends upon a more radical transformation of a site, the kind of transformations sustainable only in the realm of fantasy. One of the most adept architects of the fantasy underground is cinema scenographer Ken

Each the result of a no more
than 30-second encounter
with a complete stranger,
Eileen Perrier's photographs
of commuters were taken on
a bank of seats on the platform
of the underground Nation
RER station in Paris.

Adam. For example, in the Bond film, *You Only Live Twice* (1967), Adam fashions two superb examples of the sub-surface complex as home of the powerful: a Japanese Secret Service headquarters accessed through the lowest level of an underground car park; and a criminal nerve centre housed in a volcano, constructed on the largest studio set ever built in Europe (which used 700 tons of structural and 200 miles of tubular steel). With these buried bases, Adam attempted to 'express the neurotic electronic world we are living in which, up to then, I hadn't seen in the cinema'.[12]

Adam's cinematic constructions can be seen to be the fullest manifestation of the potential of the abstracted underground lair. However, certain developments in the real world of submerged architecture are rapidly converging with this filmic futurism. The Yates Fieldhouse at Georgetown University, Washington DC by Daniel F Tully Associates, for example, could almost be an R&R complex for SPECTRE (the Bond-film villains) with its athletics track and sports fields functioning as a roof to protect tennis courts and basketball pitches concealed underneath. Similarly, Houston, Texas's 6.3-mile system of privately-owned and maintained underground sidewalks (although they occasionally emerge as 'skywalks' to bridge the street) that connect the downtown business district represents an exercise in urban circulation that seems to resemble the set of some future-noir extrapolation of contemporary fears about the unruly street. Yet even these idiosyncratic examples of underground construction – and perhaps Adam's too – look sober in comparison to the effortless ambition of Archigram's unbuilt architecture. The Crater City project (1972) – 'Peeping from the trees. Concealed underground. Or explicit!' – as its title line indicates, proposes sinking apartments for 16,000 people around the periphery of a vast and perfect crater, balancing dramatic statement with subdued external appearance. Peter Cook's *The Metamorphosis of An English Town* suggests an emphatic response to the critique of verticality outlined above. Presented in cross-section in a sequence of successive sketches, a city is transformed from one with a typically geometric silhouette in which height retains a direct relationship with prestige, into a vegetal blob where there is only a vestige of structure visible on its soft surface. 'Eat into that tower', indeed![13]

There are many technical obstacles that assail the would-be burrower. In addition to the obvious need to establish adequate ventilation and access which is sustainable in the face of a variety of eventualities, any burrow must be shielded against the effects of moisture, negotiate existing utilities present at the site, and be reinforced against ground movements. Physical problems aside, there remains the apparent psychological impact of going underground, the spatial disorientation, claustrophobia and other documented consequences of prolonged dislocation from natural light and external views. Perhaps in an effort to eschew the effects of isolation from the sun's rays, contemporary underground accommodation frequently features a carefully-aligned glass façade (something accomplished with flair by Future System's residence for MP Bob Marshall Adams on the Pembrokeshire coast) or an arrangement of skylights (of which the domes and atriums on top of Arthur Quarmby's Mole Manor (1985) represent somewhat baroque examples). These buildings return us once again to the

12. Jane Withers, 'Sketchbook: For Your Eyes Only', *The Independent*, 6 November 1999, p.21
13. Peter Cook ed., *Archigram*, Birkhäuser Verlag, Basel 1991, pp.126–7
14. Andrea Branzi, 'No-Stop City, Residential Parking, Climatic Universal System' in Michael Hays ed., *Architectural Theory since 1968*, The MIT Press, London 2000
15. Paul Virilio and Claude Parent, *The Function of the Oblique*, Architectural Association, London 1996
16. See http://www.subbrit.org.uk

Below: the New Gourna Village near Luxor, built between 1946–53, was a key project in the career of architect Hassan Fathy, who became a champion in the West for the vernacular style and mud-brick building techniques of his native Egypt.

realm of the light-bringer. Not for their architects nor their inhabitants is 'the natural and spontaneous balance of light and air … superseded.'[14]

It is this balance which is actively sought, whether in arrangements to draw surface light below ground or in the substitution of daylight with the harsh illumination of the artificial bulb. In contrast, in the diverse troglodyte dwellings and the overground underground architecture of Fathy's and Kurokawa's projects, we see intimations of an architecture that embraces darkness as a positive force.

Bunker mentality

'Using the techniques of archaeology, I have explored the subterranean world of one of the esoteric forms of the times: the blockhouse'.[15]

The final figure of underground architecture that demands investigation is that of the military bunker. These possess a number of distinct forms. The tunnel systems dug by the Vietcong, for example, are something like the British road protestors' retreats, although any parallels are fairly superficial. Compared to the Cu Chi complex in Saigon, made up of some 200 miles of excavated channels (complete with command posts, arsenals, hospitals, educational facilities and accommodation for up to 10,000 guerrillas), the systems sunk under disputed land in Fairmile and Newbury appear fairly rudimentary. Similarly, the 'citadels' and war rooms buried underneath London could arguably be related to some of the structures associated with transport and the provision of utilities. But, again, on closer examination these security sites display a more thorough-going commitment to defensibility, autonomy and sustainability than their more innocuous counterparts. Such sites are documented through the efforts of *Subterranea Britannica*, an organisation whose energies are dedicated to mapping the the 'invisible' structures of the underground.[16] Some of these spaces are now accessible to the public, including that at Kelvedon Hatch, a subterranean labyrinth whose entrance is disguised as a rural bungalow, and which was once intended to house the government in the event of nuclear calamity – and the nuclear war command complex at Anstruther in Scotland (complete with its own broadcast facilities). Individual shelters may at first sight appear not too far distant from buried residential accommodation, yet the former demonstrate little aspiration towards comfort or (of necessity) the circulation of natural air or light. In the event of decommissioned bunkers being sold, the demands of converting it to anything approaching the standards of a conventional resident would be fairly onerous. That said, in 1999, the international press reported that defunct underground military installations were being advertised by estate agents, precisely on the basis of features which expressed their original purpose. One such property consultant specialised in what he described as 'Y2K-friendly' bunkers and announced that 'if you want to be completely safe from a nuclear attack or from chemical or biological attacks, this is the place. This home offers the ultimate in privacy and security'.

In an essay entitled 'The Geopolitics of Hibernation', published in 1962 and illustrated with a public information diagram of an apple-pie family contentedly settling down in their personal – if worryingly shallow – ▶

You park your car in a paved expanse of a parking lot and move towards the entrance of a shopping mall. Just before going in, you glance down but do not really notice a small patch of brown earth ... This small opening ... is the only visible presence of the underlying reality of the entire fabricated structure that you will momentarily become immersed in ... In the heightened, material velocity of contemporary life, shops and constructions come and go, but the ground never moves. Bill Viola

6' 5½"

Dan Tobin Smith's ongoing project to record the distinctive architectural spaces of the City of London has enabled him to collect many examples of how the financial district's almost obsessive pursuit of discretion has meant that both elevated and street-level, as well as subterranean territories adopt the defensive architectural tactics of the tunnel.

17. 'The Geopolitics of Hibernation', in Ken Knabb ed., *The Situationist International Anthology*, The Bureau of Public Secrets, Berkeley, California 1981, pp.78–9
18. Mike Davis, *City of Quartz*, Vintage, London 1992, p.223
19. Paul Virilio, *Speed and Politics*, Semiotext(e), New York 1986, p.14
20. See Paul Virilio, *The Aesthetics of Disappearance*, Semiotext(e), New York 1991, p.103
21. Paul Virilio and Claude Parent, *The Function of the Oblique*, Architectural Association, London 1996, p.13
22. *ibid* p.65
23. See Lebbeus Woods, *Radical Reconstruction*, Princeton Architectural Press, New Jersey 1997 and the synoptic overview in Angus Carlyle, 'Welcome to the War Planet' in *Themepark* Volume 1, Number 1, 2000
24. Woods, *Radical Reconstruction*, *op cit* p.16
25. Junichiro Tanizaki, *In Praise of Shadows*, Leete's Islands Books, Stony Creek, Connecticut 1977, p.18
26. Anthony Vidler, *The Architectural Uncanny: Essays on the Modern Unheimlich*, MIT Press, Cambridge, Mass. 1996, p.170
27. Ivan Chtcheglov, 'Formulary for a New Urbanism' in Ken Knabb ed., *op cit* p.2

shelter, the Situationist International delivered a devastating critique of the bunker mentality: 'The network of shelters – which are not intended for use in war, but right now – presents a still far-fetched and caricatured image of existence under a perfected bureaucratic capitalism … The world of shelters announces itself as an air-conditioned vale of tears … The subterranean sickness reveals the real nature of normal surface 'health'.[17] The Situationists contended that they were confronting a social climate in which underground bunkers distracted the post-war population from appreciating the reality that overground city life was marked by an 'urbanism of despair', that it was itself organised around a pattern of fortified and isolating cells. More recently, urban analyst Mike Davis has reinvigorated this approach in his detection of a 'militarisation of city life so grimly visible at street level'.[18] Initially focusing on Los Angeles, but then widening out to a more global frame, Davis argues that the surface of the contemporary city exhibits a 'neo-military syntax' in which space in 'introverted'. 'Residential architects are borrowing design secrets from overseas embassies and military command posts. One of the features most in demand is the 'terrorist-proof-security-room' concealed in the houseplan and accessed by sliding panels and secret doors'. Thus, the lessons learned below ground in the 'missile silos' and 'average suburban bunker' are being repeated in the upper levels of the city.

These apocalyptic analyses are supported in part by the thinking of theoriest Paul Virilio. His repeated assertion of the 'infiltration of the military's movements into daily life' encompasses the notion that the 'political triumph of the bourgeois revolution consists in spreading the state of siege of the communal city-machine, immobile in the middle of its logistic glacis and domestic lodgings, over the totality of the national territory'.[19] If Virilio later targets the colonisation of time rather than space as the military's ultimate imperative, his earlier writings nevertheless provide ample evidence that what had been developed in the underground was rising to transform the upper levels. For example, his *Bunker Archaeology*, an extended investigation of the German Atlantic Wall defences, can be read not simply as historical documentary but also as a prognosis of the future of urban space. Virilio is careful to acknowledge the aesthetic appeal of the bunker, an appeal demonstrated in Jane and Louise Wilson's enigmatic video installation *Gamma*, that slowly disinters the subterranean spaces beneath the Greenham airbases.[20] Indeed, in Virilio's own architecture, notably the Church of Sainte-Bernadette du Banlay in Nevers, France, the bunker exerts a powerful influence. His architectural manifesto attempts to respond to the 'rule' of verticality posed at the start of this essay. For Virilio, 'the traditional stability (habitable stasis) of both the rural horizontal order and the urban vertical order gave way to the Metastability of the human body in motion, in tune with the rhythms of life'.[21] 'Urbanism will in future have much more to do with ballistics than the partition of territories. In effect, the static vertical and horizontal no longer correspond to the dynamics of human life. In future, architecture must be built on the oblique, so as to accord with the new plane of human consciousness'.[22]

To encounter an architecture that engages with the diagonal as a means to disrupt the conventional axis of construction, that deploys the bunker as a design element, and forces the imperatives of the underground overground, the 'anarchitect' Lebbeus Woods remains a provocative example. Woods' unique work offers an impression of the city after the catastrophe: a structure resembling an aircraft fuselage embedded in what remains of an ordinary building, small pods raised on stilts above residential rubble, exterior surfaces latched onto host edifices like vast, rusty parasites, tracts of urban landscape engulfed by what look like poorly-constructed suits of medieval armour (all overlapping, dented metallic planes) – and the whole interwoven by a chaos of piping that looks like buried utilities brought to the surface.[23] Woods' projects present an environment in which the notion of a city level has become radically destabilised: the conventional vertical hierarchy of use has been obliterated, and replaced with no discernible logic of 'upper' or 'lower'. The orthodox delimitations of levels one from another are disrupted as whole sections of buildings are separated by precarious pillars or joined together by what amount to tunnel structures. Woods' arresting imagery and inspirational arguments (the two are inextricably integrated) betray little sense of interior space, it is the exterior that appears the primary target. This balance reflects his hostility to the programming of 'the predesigned, predetermined, predictable or predictive'[24]; the inside of what he calls freespaces 'become useful and acquire meaning only as they are inhabited', in a process of continual flux. That said, the almost total absence of transparent materials in his blueprints suggests that these habitats are unlikely to be ones in which 'natural' light contributes extensively to their occupants' experience. Instead, they are intended to embody 'architecture caught in sudden light, then broken in the continuum of darknesses' – an architecture, then, of shadows.

Hello darkness, my old friend

'And so it has come to be that the beauty of a Japanese room depends upon a variation of shadows, heavy shadows against light shadows – it has nothing else.'[25]

Approaches to the underground have frequently involved efforts to eradicate the threatening darkness, yet not all approaches to space endeavour to place it in the glare of illumination. Eighteenth-century architect Etienne Boullée for one, offers encouragement for an alternative aesthetic: 'One must, as I have tried to do in funerary monuments, present the skeleton of architecture by means of a naked wall, presenting the image of buried architecture by employing only low and compressed proportions, sinking into the earth, forming, finally, by means of materials absorbent to the light, the black picture of an architecture of shadows depicted by the effect of even blacker shadows'.[26] The Situationists, for their part, began to add new vocabulary to an architectural language of shadows. Ivan Chtcheglov (the genius originator of the unitary urbanism that underpinned the Siutationist's approach to space) rued the fact that 'darkness and obscurity are banished by artificial lighting'[27] and proposed a 'sinister quarter' in his attempt to return a measure of magic to city life.

Opposite: Effie Paleologou's
'Short History I' documents
graves uncovered during
an archaeological dig at
Spitalfields in London.

Gaston Bachelard went further still, fashioning this architectural language into a poetry of gloom in which 'the first, the oneirically definitive house must retain its shadows'.[28] For Bachelard, there is a close connection between this dimness and the territory below street level, a connection that intensifies the thoughts enabled there: 'the cellar dreamer knows that the walls of the cellar are buried walls, that they are walls with a single casing, walls that have the entire earth behind them … There, secrets are pondered, projects are prepared. And, underneath the earth, action gets underway. We are really in the intimate realm of underground manoeuvres'.[29]

There remain, of course, compelling justifications for bringing light into urban space. But need the equation of vitreous with virtuous, of illumination with perfection always apply? If room can be made for a measure of darkness in our city levels, then inspiration is already there, buried not only in the pages of poetic discourse and the plans of architecture's renegades but most emphatically in the practices of the underground itself. Troglodytes, mole people, bunker soldiers, graffiti writers, road protestors – all these people have encountered sublime shadows in their subterranean lives. Perhaps it is time their experiences were made manifest in the surface world of contemporary city.

28. Gaston Bachelard, *The Poetics of Space*, The Beacon Press, Boston, Mass. 1994, p.13
29. *ibid* p.20, 21

It is 5.30pm and commuters spill onto the Underground platform like sludge from a drain. They stand glassy-eyed and spent, buried in newspapers or half-reading the advertisements that confront them from across the track. For the time that they remain here, these people are between worlds: between home and work, between the city's urgent surface and its clammy depths, between the domesticated spaces through which our daily lives pass and the disorientation that lies at the end of the platform, waiting to swallow anyone bold enough to venture towards it.

David O'Donnell spends much of his waking life in this surreal underworld, bathed in oily half-light and clinging humidity, witnessed by weird funguses and trickles and mysterious chemical reactions that leave burning acid deposits on the walls. O'Donnell's description of the conditions he and his team of London Underground maintenance workers encounter at night sounds like a war veteran's account of the jungle in Burma, but the reality is more skewed and unnatural even than that.

There are patrols of ghostly yellow 'ballast' trains and rats the size of cats. Through years of isolation, the tunnel-dwelling mosquitoes have evolved into a distinct species. 'Fluffers' sweep for the residue of the trains' disc brakes, and of clothing and passengers' skin. 'We all adapt to the life,' O'Donnell says, 'but no one ever gets used to it.' For the three hours that the current is switched off, between two and five in the morning, an unseen army races to repair the day's damage while the population frolics or slumbers above, oblivious. And they're not alone.

Every time a Londoner flicks a switch, turns a tap or lifts a receiver, there will be a movement somewhere beneath their feet. The underground is a place of

huge, concealed bunkers, buried rivers and serpentine tangles of cables; of private railways and forgotten stations and labyrinthine networks of hidden tunnels; of miles of neo-gothic sewers and maze-like catacombs and bizarre, covered canals flowing right under Kings Cross; of hidden citadels and inverted skyscrapers over 30-storeys deep, bang in the middle of the West End. You can stand on the wire-mesh floor in one of the eight pumping stations for Thames Water's gigantic London Ring Main and beg your knees not to buckle as you hover 150 feet above a whirring, humming void. Here you feel as though you're standing at the entrance to another world, and in a sense you are. We might think of this teeming *Unterwelt* as the city's unconscious, the known but not known tributary stream running parallel to our conscious, overground, everyday lives. And some of our darkest and most extraordinary secrets are hidden here, if you know where to look.

There is an association in Britain called *Subterranea Britannica*, which claims 500 members. Ask one of its organisers, Malcolm Tadd, where his interest came from and he will tell you: 'When you go somewhere where it's dark, you're aroused, awakened, your senses become heightened. It's like us: you've got this tidy world up here, then this muddle down below. And there's always a feeling at the back of your mind that you've got to get out'. Dante, Milton and Jean Cocteau understood this. And so did the Victorians. What they feared, they either buried or sought to conquer, although sometimes they did both, which is why you might find yourself hunched, fifty feet under London's crust, thigh deep in water and waste. You'll be trying not to breathe too hard, because the atmosphere is on the foul side of acrid. They built 1,500 miles of sewer like this, making the

tunnels ingeniously egg-shaped so that the contents would run faster lower down, acquiring a scouring action in the process. London's sewerage system was the biggest engineering project of the nineteenth century and is said to still boast the finest brickwork in the world.

To visit this place is an ambivalent experience, awe mingling with desperate attempts at managing fear and claustrophobia and trying not to slip on the unspeakable ooze underfoot. But you creep along and then, suddenly, unexpectedly, the tight reflection of your torch explodes into space as you find yourself entering a huge, open chamber composed of the most immaculate red brick. Water flows everywhere, tumbling and trickling like a liquid symphony from raised shelves and fast-moving, discrete channels, to a series of sultry tributary tunnels which arc gracefully back into the darkness, smooth as a woman's hip. There are elaborate arches and flying buttresses, huge suspended iron doors, counterbalanced with 11-ton weights. Not what you might have expected, the view is part of an intricate system designed by the engineer Joseph Bazalgette, after the rank waters of the Thames caused the 'Great Stink' of 1858. The result is a neo-Gothic masterpiece: unseen, little known, but breathtaking.

Sewermen tell tales of old timers who know where slight

irregularities in the walls cause treasure to catch. They will admit that these might be apocryphal. 'We get everything down here,' smiles one, but mostly they get jewellery and guns, buried in silt. Sometimes, they run across dead animals, occasionally people; once, there was a baby. John and his colleagues find the things we don't want in the 'civilised' world above. No wonder then that their domain has provided such a ready metaphor for evil, or, in modern times, dissent. The fascination, the perturbation, is probably as old as humanity itself. And as strong as ever. There is a story that the planners of the Jubilee Line extension to the London Underground had their projected route under Westminster rejected several times. They were bemused. No obstructions were shown on the official drawings and no-one would explain quite what the problem was. Naturally, there is a theory about this. A member of the Research Study Group, who concern themselves with documenting the constructions of the Cold War era, offers the view that, 'The situation around Parliament Square is still very uncertain. There is a lot going on, but we don't really know what it is ... the rumour is that there is a vast bunker down there, which the government has kept secret, that is the grand-daddy of them all.' The investigative journalist Duncan Campbell, has looked into the Parliament Square mystery,

INTO DARK SPACE
ANDREW SMITH

and thinks he has come close to the truth, 'What I didn't previously know was that the government had built two huge bunkers since the War. One was the hydrogen bomb citadel near Bath. But I didn't spot three clues as to the A-bomb measures. That does amount to a city under London. What fascinates me is that the scale of what was done underneath central London had not been calculated.'

Still we don't know for sure. We can't see, are forced to rely, as always in the dark, on our imaginations and the distensions that take place there. Nevertheless, we do know that the space under our feet is riven with secret and not-so secret tunnel systems, bunkers, shelters and underground buildings constructed during World War II and the Cold War. Before the War, service corporations had already begun to amass subterranean empires, but the first serious government-sponsored schemes were begun in the 1930s, when the cabinet authorised the construction of 12 miles of tunnel, linking interconnected war rooms and eight massive 'citadels', 100 feet under the ground. A decade later in 1949, the detonation of Russia's first nuclear bomb sparked a fevered second wave of planning, which resulted in the biggest subterranean building project since Bazalgette's sewers. Fear of the unknown had again driven us to ground. Even now, night workers on the Underground frequently

stumble across doors which appear to lead nowhere, but don't.

In fact, Chamberlain's government had begun the War determined not to provide deep shelters for the public. Londoners were also instructed not to use tube stations for shelter, but they bought the cheapest possible ticket and went down anyway. At its peak, 170,000 people were virtually living in what became makeshift communities, with canteens and libraries. Stumbling across them, the sculptor Henry Moore made a series of sketches of what he saw, images which the writer Iain Sinclair describes as looking 'like incubating dreams under the city'. Eventually, London County Council dug six trenches for its citizens, the largest at Finsbury, which could hold 12,000 people, and is now a dusty and nondescript underground car park. The government also succumbed to the pressure to provide deep-level facilities, building shelters for

8,000 people each underneath tube stations at Belsize Park, Camden Town, Goodge Street, Chancery Lane, Stockwell, Clapham North, Clapham Common and Clapham South; completed in 1943, only four were actually opened to the public. Goodge Street became the headquarters of General Eisenhower, Chancery Lane an invasion citadel (for use if London was overrun), and Stockwell a US troops' hostel. All still exist.

As they step into the high-speed lift and plunge downward, the visitor to the shelter at Goodge Street – the 'Eisenhower Tower' – will realise that they are entering what amounts to a 32-storey inverted skyscraper. The entrance, located in Chenies Street, just off Tottenham Court Road, is contained in a large, cylindrical shaft that looms over passers-by on the pavement. It leads to a deep maze of unnervingly long, seemingly infinite walkways. Now leased from the government

by Security Archives Ltd, some of the gloomy, branching chambers are used to store valuable documents: there are unreleased John Lennon recordings, sheaves of confiscated child pornography, BBC materials and unspecified items deposited by private individuals. Others sectors have been left as they were when US troops were billeted in them. The ancient machinery, with its *Dr Who*-like proliferation of knobs and dials and fluorescent cathode-ray tubes, combined with soldiers' homesick graffiti, is strangely evocative in these murky surroundings. Your own unease seems to chime with that of the young men who left it there. You find yourself simultaneously eager to explore and desperate to leave, yearning for the safety of the surface yet lured by the seductive promise of the unknown, of depth.

Reputedly, a clause in the letting agreement for the Eisenhower Tower allows the government to regain possession at any time, with no notice. And such is the pact we make with the underground. This is where we place our dead, lay our ghosts, bury our past. It is where creatures with no need of sight or fear writhe through a world created and defined by decay, feeding on each other, one day to feed on us. We may be gifted a glimpse of the other side, but only at its discretion. Once underground, everything seems contingent – we may be reclaimed at any time.

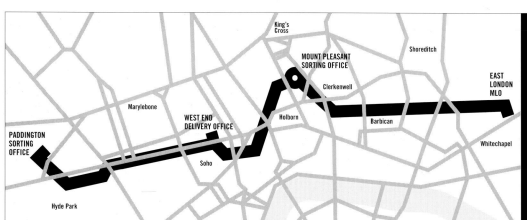

Every day, 4 million letters and parcels are transported between London's main sorting offices via a unique underground railway system. The world's first fully-automated train service, 'Mail Rail' was conceived by the Postmaster General in 1909 and in operation by 1927. Today, 50 computer-controlled trains (each capable of pulling 10 tonnes), run along 37 kilometres of track for 19 hours a day. These deliveries, at least, never get stuck in a traffic jam.

A disused train depot at Bishopsgate under the City of London. Above opposite: the disused 'ghost station' at Down Street on the London Underground.

Part of a series of photographs documenting Hong Kong, taken by Ralph Kamena.

THE TUNNEL
MARGARET MORTON